PENGUIN HANDBOOKS PH96

Cacti and other Succulents

R. GINNS

R. Ginns was educated at Wellingborough School and proceeded to Manchester University in 1914, but his studies were interrupted by the First World War. He served with the Royal Engineers in France and was commissioned in the Indian army with which he served in Baluchistan, Persia, and Afghanistan where his interest in desert plants was aroused.

Later he obtained a B.Sc. at London University, and became a teacher of science and finally head of the science department of Kettering Central School. Mr Ginns joined the National Cactus and Succulent Society in its early days, became secretary of the Shows Committee, and later joined the editorial advisory panel of the society's *Journal*. He has travelled extensively to study succulents, both wild and cultivated, and was elected Fellow of the Society in 1961.

The cover illustration shows an old plant of *Mammillaria albilanata* (centre), a *Gymnocalcium* (on right, below), a cristate cactus (above), and lower parts of an *Oreocereus* and a *Cereus* (in background).

Greenhouse collection of succulents

R. GINNS

Cacti
and other succulents

*Prepared in conjunction and collaboration
with the Royal Horticultural Society*

PENGUIN BOOKS

Penguin Books Ltd, Harmondsworth, Middlesex
AUSTRALIA: Penguin Books Pty Ltd, 762 Whitehorse Road,
Mitcham, Victoria

First published 1963

Copyright © R. Ginns, 1963

Made and printed in Great Britain
by Jarrold and Sons Ltd, Norwich

Set in Monotype Times New Roman

Contents

List of Plates

List of Text Figures

Acknowledgements

In the following pages all descriptions are taken from my own plants grown at Desborough, Northamptonshire, and all are obtainable from the many nurseries which specialize in succulents.

Photographs by the following are included and their help and skill is acknowledged with many thanks: Mr B. Alfieri, Mr P. R. Chapman, Mr J. E. Downward, Mr J. Ireson, Mr S. Littlewood, Miss M. J. Martin, Mr D. Paterson, Mr G. W. Robinson, Mr H. Smith, and Mrs C. Woolston and W. F. Sedgwick Ltd. The picture of *Selenicereus grandiflorus* is reproduced from the *Temple of Flora*, 1800. The figures were drawn by Mr W. Bartram.

I must also gratefully acknowledge the encouragement given me by my many friends in the National Cactus and Succulent Society and, in particular, the help afforded by my wife in correcting and typing the manuscript.   R. G.

Introduction

It was early in the 1930s that, wandering round a well-known multiple store, I came across a number of strange-looking plants in tiny pots on sale at 6d each. I was so fascinated by them that I bought a number. This was my first acquaintance with succulents. My interest in them grew apace, and by the time that war broke out I had several hundreds. With no possibility of heating a greenhouse and several very cold winters, most of these plants were lost, but when the war at last came to an end I collected together the few survivors and set about adding to them.

For a considerable time this was not easy as nurserymen had lost their stocks, and exchange difficulties prevented importation. Gradually conditions improved, and more and more species of succulents came on the market. Many of those not available from the nurseries were raised from seed. Today I have in the region of 1,500 species.

Most of these plants can today be bought from the specialist nurseries or from the ever-increasing number of dealers who obtain plants collected from their native deserts. It is not possible in this book to describe more than a very small proportion of the many thousands of species known, but all those mentioned can be obtained from commercial sources in this country.

These plants have a very strong attraction for an expanding circle of admirers, and by following certain relatively simple rules a most interesting collection may be grown either in a small greenhouse or even in a sunny window. The novice should not be too ambitious in his choice of plants: it is a mistake to start with expensive specimens; but by starting with a score or so of easy species he can get a good idea of what is involved, after which an attempt may be made with more difficult ones.

Popularity of Succulents

In addition to the ability of many succulents to withstand a considerable amount of neglect, there are other reasons which account for their undoubted popularity. The symmetrical shapes of cacti and the geometrical patterns of their spines blend well with modern architecture and furniture. In fact, we can consider them as 'contemporary', using the word in the same way as it is applied to furnishing and interior decoration. Maybe the more grotesque of the cacti such as *Lophocereus schottii*, *Cereus peruvianus monstrosus*, *Aztekium*, and many of the cristate forms provide a good foil for abstract paintings, their forms having as little resemblance to normal plants as the paintings have to the outward appearance of their subjects.

Miniatures appeal to many people, particularly children, and many can be obtained and grown for a considerable time in two-inch or even smaller pots. Thus quite a varied collection can be kept in the small area of a window-sill. Children are fascinated by these tiny plants and some become expert growers whilst still in their teens.

The very large number of different species available also appeals to the collecting instinct most of us have. The acquisition of a rare specimen gives the hardened collector of succulents as big a thrill as a philatelist gets when he meets with a rare stamp.

Finally, many of the commoner succulents are so easily propagated by leaves or stem cuttings that bits are given away by people growing them to visitors and so another enthusiast is born.

What is a Succulent?

The dictionary tells us that 'succulent' means 'juicy'. Thus succulent plants are those in which one or more organs are adapted to contain a juicy tissue. In this tissue the plant is able to store water when it is freely available in order to be able to draw on it when external supplies are short. The French name, *plantes grasses*, literally 'fat plants', emphasizes the way in which certain parts of the plant are swollen in order to contain this water-storing tissue. This tissue may be contained either in the stem or in the leaves, and succulent plants are therefore divided into stem succulents or leaf succulents.

Not only are these plants able to store water for use during periods of drought, but they also have various exterior modifications which prevent excessive loss of moisture by transpiration

– that is, the escape of excess water from the plant through tiny holes, usually in the leaves, known as stomata. In many succulents, such as most cacti and stapeliads and many euphorbias, the number of these stomata is drastically reduced by the disappearance of the leaves, the normal functions of the leaves being performed by the stems, though many stem succulents do still retain their leaves. Escape of water from the reduced number of stomata is also made more difficult by a covering of waxy material, often glaucous blue in colour; by a thick coating of farina (flour), particularly noticeable in the *Dudleyas* (Pl. 106); or by a more or less thick network of hairs or spines. These differences from normal plants, to enable them to live under conditions of drought, give succulents their chief interest and beauty, and, as they become less prominent when the plants receive an abundance of food and water, it is well to bear this in mind when considering their cultivation.

These arrangements for conserving water in addition to the possession of water-storing tissues are the real mark of those plants suitable for growing in succulent collections. Quite a number of plants (for example, begonias) have very juicy stems, but are not considered to be succulents as their large leaves transpire freely and they are quite unable to withstand a shortage of water for even short periods. On the other hand, some plants perfectly suitable for growing in succulent collections cannot, under any circumstances, be looked upon as juicy. I have in mind some of the agaves, a very large genus. While the leaves of the commonly grown *Agave americana* are thick and fleshy, those of *A. stricta* and others are long, narrow, and rigid, like so many needles. Many of the bromeliads, such as *Billbergia*, whose leaves are quite thin, are also quite satisfied with the conditions provided for more fleshy-leaved subjects.

The ability of succulents to survive when left untended for a considerable length of time is one of the reasons why these plants are so suitable for house decoration. It is possible to go away and leave them for a week or more without water and on returning find them still flourishing. In fact, they will do far better with little water than with an excess, which can well be fatal.

1. Areoles of *Mammillaria compressa*
showing cushions with wool and spines

What is a Cactus?

Whilst succulents have been known in this country for over three and a half centuries, it is only during the present century that they have attained the degree of popularity they now possess. Owing to an imperfect knowledge of the conditions under which they grow wild, a number of misconceptions have arisen concerning them. The first of these concerns their naming. It is common to hear all succulents referred to as 'cacti'. Whilst all cacti are succulents, considerably more than half the known species of succulents are not cacti. Plants are divided into families based on the characteristics of the flowers, and the cacti form one of these families, the botanical name for which is the *Cactaceae*. Many other families consist entirely of, or contain, succulent plants – such as the euphorbia, lily, crassula, and mesembryanthemum families. When these flower the difference between them and cacti is at once apparent. Apart from the mesembryanthemums and stapelias, few of the other succulents commonly grown have large showy flowers such as the cacti have.

Many people get into difficulties over 'cactus', 'cacti', and

2. Areoles and spines of *Mammillaria herrerae*, which entirely hide the plant body, much enlarged

'cactuses', not knowing which to use. 'Cactus' is singular and 'cacti' is the grammatically correct plural, although 'cactuses', according to a modern dictionary, can also be used as the plural. Thus we should say 'one cactus' but 'two cacti'.

As many of the cacti grown in our collections can never become large enough to flower, the flower characteristics are of little use for us to decide whether a particular plant is a 'cactus' or not. There is, however, another distinction. All cacti possess a remarkable vegetative organ found in no other plant family. This is the areole, a small cushion of woolly felt or hair from which the spines arise (Pl. 1). Areoles occur in the axils of leaves, or the places where leaves would have been, and may possibly represent a transformed side-shoot. We have in nature what is known as 'parallel development' where plants of totally different families under similar climatic conditions develop into very similar vegetative forms. Thus some of the tall growing *Cerei* (Cacti) (Pl. 26) and *Euphorbias* are almost indistinguishable to the non-botanist, but a cursory examination will show the areoles present on a *Cereus* but their complete absence on a *Euphorbia*.

Even when it is realized that some succulents are not cacti, there are other misconceptions. I have seen it stated by a well-known gardener that 'cacti have spines but no leaves, whilst other succulents have leaves but no spines'. The absurdity of this statement will be realized by anyone with even a small representative collection of succulents, and can be seen from the illustrations in this book. Amongst cacti the *Pereskias* (Pl. 27) have well-developed, persistent leaves and many of the *Opuntias* have small leaves on the young shoots, while *Zygocactus*, *Epiphyllums*, and *Rhipsalis* are totally spineless. On the other hand, among succulents that are not cacti we find many *Euphorbias* without leaves but with quite powerful spines, while among the very large family of *Stapeliads* only a single member, *Freeria indica*, possesses leaves.

People often speak of the leaves of *Epiphyllums* (Pls. 75 and 76) and *Zygocactus* (Pl. 4). This is still another misconception, as what are sometimes considered to be leaves are in reality flattened stems, which can easily be seen when the plant is in flower. In the case of *Zygocactus* the flower appears at the end of the leaf-like stem; in the *Epiphyllums* a number of flowers are carried along the edge of the flattened stems. In no case in the floral world are flowers produced on the leaves. With *Epiphyllums* it is true that some of the growths are rounded and some three-sided, but whatever the shape they are all stems. This diversity is explained by the hybrid origin of most *Epiphyllums*, plants of a number of different vegetative shapes having taken part in their ancestry.

Flowering of Succulents

Another commonly held misconception is that succulents flower only every seven years. It is impossible to know why the seven came to be chosen, though it is quite correct that certain succulents, or near-succulents such as *Yuccas*, take several years between flowering periods. This is only the case with some rosette-forming plants which flower from the centre of the rosette. In most cases when this happens the flowering rosette dies, as can be seen in the case of all the *Sempervivums* (Pl. 3). If no offsets have been produced before flowering, of course the whole plant dies. A classic example of this is *Agave americana*, at one time known

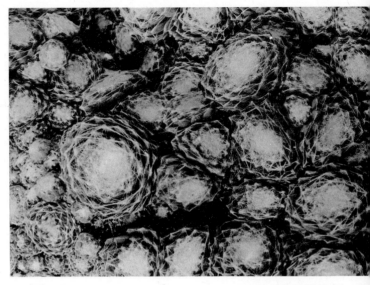

3. *Sempervivum arachnoideum* showing network of hairs giving rise to name of 'Cobweb Houseleek'

as the 'Century Plant'. This was supposed to grow for a hundred years before flowering and dying. Actually, it takes from ten to fifteen years for the rosette to become strong enough to produce its huge flowering spike. The *Yuccas* either produce basal offsets, which enable the plant to carry on after the flowering rosette has died, or else two buds are formed below the flower spike which in time grow into flowering rosettes themselves, hence the branching habit of species like *Yucca gloriosa*. Again, it takes several years for these rosettes to become strong enough to flower, the time taken depending on conditions of soil, water, and temperature. But there is no justification for the choice of seven years as the time taken.

However, the majority of succulents will flower every year once they have attained maturity and provided they have suitable conditions. In the case of cacti, this matter of maturity requires some elaboration. The cacti are a very large family, with 220 genera according to Backeberg's latest classification, and, of course, with several thousand different species. These genera vary from tiny plants less than an inch high to huge plants that can take their place among forest trees, and it is obvious that the small ones will flower much sooner than the big ones. With the most suitable conditions it is possible to have *Rebutias* and *Mammillarias* flowering the year following seed sowing, but obviously the giants like *Carnegia* and *Pachycereus* take many years to reach flowering size. In fact, without a greenhouse the size of the Palm House at Kew, it is doubtful whether these can ever be flowered in this country.

Still, once a cactus has bloomed, there is no reason why it should not flower every year. A hint as to the conditions most suitable for the production of flowers on cacti can be gathered from the fact that in 1960, after the very dry summer of 1959, a very wide variety of cacti flowered in my collection, many of them for the first time. Flowers on cacti can be expected from May, when the *Rebutias* and *Mammillarias* start, until August, but even after that odd flowers will be produced. Some *Rhipsalis* normally flower in late autumn and, of course, *Zygocactus truncatus* (Pl. 4), the so-called 'Christmas Cactus', will flower during that season as the name implies. There is also an 'Easter Cactus'.

Flowers can be expected from the other succulents at all times of the year. Many *Aloes* bloom in autumn and the same can be said of many of the *Mesembryanthemums*, for example *Lithops*, *Conophytums*, *Argyrodermas*, *Faucarias*, *Pleiospilos*, and so on. A carefully chosen selection of succulents will provide colour in the greenhouse all the year round.

Starting a Collection

The range of species now readily available from growers is so large that those thinking of starting a collection may have some difficulty in deciding which plants to obtain first. Among the cacti some *Mammillarias* should certainly be included. These are relatively small-growing and free-flowering and can be obtained with a wide variety of spine colours and formations. Next in popularity are the *Rebutias*, *Aylosteras*, and *Mediolobivias*, which give large, brightly coloured flowers when quite small. *Echinopses* are easy to

4. *Zygocactus truncatus* showing flattened branches
which look like leaves

look after, producing their lovely long-tubed flowers under
window-sill conditions. Other floriferous genera that do not take
up much space are *Astrophytum*, *Chamaecereus*, *Gymnocalycium*,
Lobivia, *Notocactus*, and *Parodia*.

To vary the height of the collection some *Cerei*, *Cephalocerei*,
Cleistocacti, *Espostoas*, and *Haageocerei* may be included. These
can be obtained with white, golden, red, or brown spines, often
with long white hair, but they are most unlikely to flower.
Opuntias are not recommended as they take up a lot of room,
seldom flower, and are difficult to handle. They should never be
grown within reach of young children as the fine spines (glochids)
from the areoles come away in the fingers and are difficult to
remove.

The finest flowering cacti of all are the *Epiphyllums*, which are
very suitable as window plants. Closely allied and also desirable
are *Zygocactus* and *Aporocactus*.

Many fascinating rarities, collected in the deserts of America
and imported into this country, are now available. These should

not be attempted until commoner plants can be successfully grown. They are expensive and often cannot be induced to form new roots.

Besides cacti some of the other succulents should certainly be included in any collection. Foremost here are the *Echeverias*, rosette-forming plants with leaf colouring ranging over almost the entire spectrum and often with showy, long-lasting flowers. *Crassulas* should not be neglected but need choosing with care as some are difficult to keep. There are, however, numerous small-growing, free-flowering species. *Gasterias*, with long tongue-shaped leaves, and *Haworthias*, with rosettes of often prettily marked leaves, are attractive and easy. Most *Agaves* and *Aloes* grow too large for inclusion in a small collection, although *Aloe variegata* is a popular window plant. Some *Euphorbias*, very similar to cacti in appearance, are easy but are negligible from the flowering point of view. All the *Stapelias* have most unusual flowers, but are not very interesting when out of bloom.

All the mesembryanthemums have showy flowers. The many shrubby species are easy and some suitable for bedding out. But the very succulent genera, such as *Lithops*, *Conophytum*, *Gibbaeum*, and others need expert care and should not be attempted as window plants. Less extreme forms such as *Faucaria*, *Pleiospilos*, and *Titanopsis* may be grown by beginners.

Fuller details of all these plants will be found in the classified list in the second part of this book (from page 69). The ones suggested here can be obtained as small plants at about 2s 6d each.

1 · The habitats of succulent plants

A knowledge of the area from which any particular plant comes can be of considerable help to us when deciding on the kind of soil, temperature, amount of water, and so on that it needs.

It is widely believed that succulents, particularly cacti, are to be found only in the most arid deserts. This is far from being the case as they in fact appear in most climatic regions, even in the tropical forests which are regions of very heavy rainfall. Indeed, vast areas of sandy deserts are devoid of succulents as the shifting sand would bury them; and in regions like the Sahara, Arabian, Gobi, Indian, and Australian Deserts such plants as there are have adopted other methods of coping with the excessive dryness – with a few exceptions.

In the Sahara and in Arabia there are a few species of *Aloes*, *Euphorbias*, and *Stapeliads* whose range also extends into the Atlas Mountains of Morocco. In Australia there are a few of the less interesting species of *Mesembryanthemum*. The numerous specimens of *Opuntias* found all round the Mediterranean are descendants of plants introduced there after the discovery of America. *Opuntias* are also very common in Australia, where they are a serious pest. In the high mountain ranges of Europe and Asia are to be found the succulent *Sempervivums*, *Sedums*, *Orostachys*, and similar plants, but as these are hardy on our rock gardens they are not usually grown in our collections of succulents, although *Sempervivum arachnoideum* (Pl. 3), the spider's web *Sempervivum*, is sometimes offered in the shops and is often referred to as a cactus.

Apart from these few plants the great majority of our succulents come to us from North and South America and southern Africa.

Cacti come almost exclusively from the Americas. The only exceptions are a few species of *Rhipsalis* which are found in West Africa, India, Ceylon, and Mauritius as well as in South America. Opinion is divided as to whether they are native there or were introduced by birds. In America the family extends from the prairies of Canada to the sheep farms of Patagonia.

In Canada only a few species are found, including the low-growing *Opuntia polyacantha* and *Coryphantha vivipara* in British Columbia and Alberta, where they are deeply covered by snow during the winter. It might be thought that they would be suitable for outdoor cultivation in this country but our wet winters and alternate frost and thaw usually kill them when planted outside. Not a great many species are found in the northern and eastern states of the U.S.A. *Pediocactus simpsonii* and *Neobesseya missouriensis* are examples of those that are. In southern California, Arizona, Texas, and New Mexico the number of species rapidly increases, and *Opuntias*, *Mammillarias*, *Echinocerei*, *Echinocacti*, and *Ferocacti* are found in particular. These latter two genera attain a very large size and are known as 'barrel cacti'. In these areas, too, we have the giant saguero, *Carnegia gigantea*, whose huge trunks and often strangely contorted branches form a conspicuous feature of the landscape.

Passing south into Mexico we find in its vast semideserts a bigger variety of genera and species than in any other country. This is the home of the greater number of the very numerous species of *Mammillaria*. On the dry, slaty slopes of the state of Hidalgo are found serried ranks of *Cephalocereus senilis* (Pl. 32), the very popular 'Old Man Cactus', many of them over two hundred years old. Elsewhere are to be found other giant columnar cerei such as *Pachycereus* and *Lemaireocereus*. In the state of Baja California conditions of extreme drought are experienced, and the cacti from this region need extra care in watering. From here come *Lophocereus schottii*, the 'Totem Pole Cactus', and *Machaerocereus eruca*, the 'Creeping Devil'.

In southern Mexico and central America the rainfall increases whilst the temperature remains consistently high. This favours the development of dense forests in place of the deserts and semideserts farther north. The forests in places are so thick that small plants are absent from the ground, and in order to reach the light have taken to growing on trees. The roots of such plants do not, like the mistletoe, penetrate the tissues of the host plant but grow in the accumulations of humus found in the forks of branches and cracks in the bark. It is from such humus that the plant draws its food supplies while water is absorbed from the moist atmosphere by means of aerial roots which are very conspicuous on some species of *Selenicereus* (Pl. 38) in our collections. These plants are known as epiphytes. Many orchids adopt the same habit of growth, and I have seen collections of epiphytic cacti grown in the same way as orchids in hanging baskets filled with sphagnum moss. Other species have their roots in the ground, but have a climbing habit and can be seen scrambling to the tops of tall palm trees. Prominent among these forest plants are species of *Epiphyllum*, *Hylocereus*, *Rhipsalis*, *Schlumbergera*, and *Zygocactus*. None of these exhibit extreme succulence as they do not have to contend with prolonged drought. As, too, the atmosphere is seldom dry and drying winds are absent, these plants have no need of the spines and hairs to be found on the desert cacti. The number of different species shows a marked diminution as we move south from Mexico to Panama.

The West Indian islands have their cacti, many of which are confined to single islands. There are mammillarias, opuntias, and a variety of the tall, columnar cerei. In particular there is the plant that gave its name to the whole family, named *Cactus* by Linnaeus but renamed *Melocactus* by Schumann and generally known as 'Turk's Cap Cactus'. All plants from this region are accustomed to a warm, moist atmosphere, which should be borne in mind when growing them.

In the drier forests of eastern Brazil are to be found many columnar cacti belonging to the genera *Cereus*, *Pilocereus*, *Cephalocereus*, *Eriocereus*, *Monvillea*, and others. These may either take their place as trees among the other trees in the forest, or else form small shrubs in the undergrowth, or scramble over the other vegetation.

On the western side of the Andes in South America we find a totally different cactus population. In much of Peru and Bolivia conditions are very dry, and in parts the vegetation depends almost entirely for its existence on mists and dew. Many cacti grow right up to the snow-line and are well fitted to withstand dry cold. On the mountain slopes we find groves of tall *Espostoas* and *Oreocerei*. These differ markedly from the columnar species of

23

the eastern part of the continent by the amount of hair and the closeness of the spine formations. They are thus far more worth a place in our collections. On the high plateau between the main ranges are many very hairy *Opuntias*. There are also globular plants belonging to the genera *Matucana*, *Mila*, *Oroya*, and *Lobivia*. Much of this area is still being explored botanically, and every year new species of these genera are being introduced to cultivation. The travels of Herr Ritter are bringing these plants, some of the most beautiful of the smaller cacti, within reach of all growers of cacti.

As we move south from Peru the mountains approach closer to the sea, and the climate gets still drier until in the Atacama Desert of northern Chile an entirely waterless region is reached. *Browningias* and *Eulychnias* are the columnar forms in this area whilst *Copiapoas* and *Neoporterias* are low-growing. All are beautiful, but in view of their habitat need extreme care when being watered.

Across the Andes are the dry-grass regions of northern Argentina which are particularly rich in cactus species, mostly low-growing. A study of *Rebutias* and their allies seems to indicate that cacti are still in process of evolution in this area. *Chamaecereus*, *Gymnocalyciums*, *Notocacti*, *Trichocerei*, and *Echinopses* all come from this region. As these plants get protection from the sun by means of the grass amongst which they grow it is obvious that they require different treatment from the *Copiapoas* and *Neoporterias* growing in the totally bare deserts across the Andes. Certain species of these genera extend across the continent into Paraguay and Uruguay. They are joined by the taller-growing *Cleistocacti*. Even on the scrub-covered hills of Patagonia a few cacti are to be found, chiefly the short-jointed forms of *Opuntia*, sometimes separated as *Tephrocactus*, and the leafy, cushion-forming *Maihuenias*.

The Galapagos Islands, out in the Pacific, have *Brachycereus* and *Jasminocereus*, tall-growing species seldom seen in collections in Great Britain.

It must not be thought that all succulents in America are cacti. *Agaves*, like cacti, were once confined to America but are now common features of the Mediterranean landscape. In East Africa

24

they are cultivated extensively for the production of sisal fibre. In America they are most frequently found in Mexico, where they are cultivated for an alcoholic drink which can be produced from the sap.

Mexico and the dry regions of southern California are the chief home of the numerous colourful species of *Echeveria* and the closely related *Pachyphytums* and *Dudleyas*. Also in the mountains of Mexico are to be found many low-growing and also shrubby species of *Sedums*. In Baja California are to be seen the weird *Idria columnaris*, known locally as boojum trees, while considerable succulence is shown by a number of other less well-known trees and shrubs.

The many species of bromeliads found all over the warmer regions of America, both terrestrial and epiphytic, are adapted to withstand drought and can be grown in collections of succulents without modifying the conditions. Opinions differ as to which of them can be considered as succulents, but, apart from occasions when they are put in shows, this is a matter of personal opinion. The brilliant colours and unusual shapes make them, in my opinion, a welcome addition to a collection of the more common species.

In the Old World most of the well-known succulents come from the Union of South Africa. There, a narrow coastal belt bounded by mountains is fertile. Beyond the mountains is the Karroo, with a much drier climate and with vast areas covered with low-growing bushes. It is under these bushes that many species of succulents are found, since in this way they receive shade from the burning sun when they are in a young and tender state. Also, proceeding north from Cape Town along the west coast, the climate becomes progressively drier through Namaqualand, home of many rare succulents, until at Walfisch Bay, chief port of south-west Africa, there is a region of waterless sand-dunes, quite devoid of vegetation. Inland from there is the Kalahari Desert where *Pachypodiums* and *Welwitchias* are to be found.

Eastwards from Cape Town along the coast the rainfall increases as far as Natal, where I was told the climate is really too wet for good results to be obtained with succulents. But not far inland, in the Zulu Reserve, I found the landscape dominated

5. *Aloe striata* growing in South Africa

by large aloes (Pls. 5 and 6) and euphorbias. The latter grew thickly enough to cover large areas.

The dry mountain-sides north of Cape Town are a succulent-lover's paradise. Amongst the rocks are many species of *Aloe, Cotyledon, Othonna, Crassula, Mesembryanthemum*, and succulent *Pelargonium*. In crevices at the tops of the range are *Conophytums* and *Crassulas*. Beyond, on the Karroo, are *Haworthias, Gasterias, Cotyledons, Euphorbias, Stapeliads*, and *Mesembryanthemums*.

The many kinds of dwarf, extremely succulent, mesembryanthemums such as *Lithops, Fenestrarias, Argyrodermas*, and so on are found in still drier, more open country. Much of the landscape is dominated by tree aloes (Pl. 6), and in various parts of the Union are to be found scores of species of *Aloe, Haworthia, Adromiscus*, and *Crassula*.

The thorn forests of East Africa have *Aloes, Euphorbias, Stapeliads*, and a large variety of caudiciform species, with their fantastic-looking swollen stems, from a number of plant families. Madagascar also has many strange plants, including *Kalanchoes* and *Euphorbias*.

Lastly, mention must be made of the Canary Islands from whence come the *Aeoniums* (Pls. 100 and 101), *Monanthes*, and similar genera.

6. *Aloe dichotoma* and *Cotyledon paniculata* near Steinkopf in South Africa

7. *Hoodia bainii* growing near Calvinia in South Africa

2 · Cultivation

(A) *Containers*

In this country most succulents must be grown under cover in either a greenhouse, frame, or the windows of a house. Thus containers of some kind must in most cases be used. By far the greatest number of succulents are grown in unglazed earthenware pots, the traditional receptacle for the growth of greenhouse and house plants. The disadvantage of these pots is that they soon become dirty through the formation of a white incrustation of lime on the outside. So, whenever a plant is repotted, the old pot should be soaked in rain-water for a few days, and then the incrustation can be easily removed with a scrubbing brush.

Recently plastic pots in a variety of bright colours have appeared on the market. These are very useful for plants grown in houses as the exterior always looks clean. It is claimed for them that plants grow better in them than in clay pots and, as there is no evaporation through the sides, not so much watering is needed. But they are considerably more expensive than clay pots, and this is definitely a consideration to be borne in mind when a large number of plants are grown in greenhouses. It is not advisable to use both clay and plastic pots in a greenhouse as the watering technique for the two kinds is so different.

In America, use is made of tins. These should have the same advantages as plastic pots, but from the point of view of appearance alone I should hesitate to use them. Where there is plenty of greenhouse space, plants can be planted in prepared beds of porous, gritty compost and their rate of growth enormously increased. When this is done, discretion must be exercised in the choice of varieties, as some *Opuntias*, *Euphorbias*, and others, soon occupy a very large area and are liable to smother less vigorous species.

(B) *Soil*

There is much conflict of opinion among growers as to the best compost to use. But everyone must agree that certain properties

8. Greenhouse collection of cacti

are essential. It must, for example, have an open texture to allow rapid drainage. For this, plenty of sharp sand or broken brick is needed; a water-logged soil would quickly prove fatal to all but the most robust species. On the other hand, it should not dry out too quickly, so it is a good idea to add granulated peat or leaf mould to retain some of the water. The question of nourishment must not be forgotten, so a good loam must be used. The old idea of growing cacti in a mixture consisting of little more than sand and broken brick has been largely discarded. A good general mixture consists of equal parts of medium loam, granulated peat or leaf mould, and sharp sand. (Builders' sand is not suitable.) To this can be added a sprinkling of bone-meal and a small amount of old mortar rubble, or crushed limestone in the case of desert cacti, to assist in strong spine formation. Those without facilities for mixing their own compost should purchase John Innes Compost Number 1, obtainable from most seedsmen, which has been proved most suitable for the cultivation of the majority of succulents.

Forest cacti, such as *Epiphyllums, Heliocereus, Selenicereus, Rhipsalis,* and so on, require, however, a richer compost, with a greater proportion of leaf mould, their natural food. Lime should be avoided for these as they are accustomed to an acid medium.

The question of artificial feeding sometimes arises. I have sometimes heard the use of liquid nitrogenous manures advocated. But this leads to rapid, soft growth, usually of an unnatural deep green colour, and unless the cultivator is an expert, plants may be lost through rotting. Special mixtures of salts have been produced especially for cacti and these can be used, carefully following the maker's instructions, if more rapid growth is needed. Actually, however, the John Innes Compost will provide all that the majority of plants require.

It should be realized that the foregoing applies to the majority of plants in the average collection. There are plants from special habitats which require special composts. In such cases, instructions will be found in the descriptions in Chapter 10.

(c) *Potting*

It is important to choose pots the right size for the plants. They should not be too large as the roots of a small plant fail to fill the pot, with the result that the unused soil has a tendency to become sour. On the other hand, if the pot is too small it becomes filled with a mass of roots and watering is made difficult; the plant is also starved so that its growth is checked. The very tiny pots sometimes offered for cacti are not to be recommended as they dry out too quickly. Of course, if space is limited underpotting may be necessary to restrict the plant size to the space available. This is particularly the case with large-growing plants like some of the *Opuntias* and *Aloes*.

Plenty of broken crocks should be placed in the bottom of the pots so that the drainage hole does not become blocked. A few pieces of charcoal can be mixed with the crocks to help to keep the soil sweet. Also, if there is any likelihood of root mealy bugs, a few crystals of paradichlorobenzene, available from any chemist, may be added.

The roots of the plant should be well spread out in the pot, and the compost sifted amongst them and afterwards firmed down to keep the plant steady. But this firming should not be excessive as it might interfere with the rapid drainage necessary. The soil should not reach higher than a third of an inch below the rim of the pot.

To prevent the growth of moss on the surface of the soil, a top dressing of chippings is useful. A neutral-coloured stone such as granite is preferable to the highly coloured bits sometimes seen, as it displays the plant better. In the case of mimicking plants such as *Lithops*, larger pieces of stone similar in colour to the plant look well, tending to emphasize the mimicry.

The plants should be repotted each year as early in the growing season as possible. Old soil should be shaken off the roots and any broken or decayed roots carefully trimmed. Plants that flower early, such as *Rebutias*, should have the repotting delayed until after flowering, as once buds have formed the plant should not be disturbed. While most plants start their growing period in spring others become dormant in summer and grow during the autumn and winter. (Where this is the case it is noted in the list of plants later in the book.) After repotting, no water should be given for some days so that any broken roots can heal over, otherwise the roots may rot.

(D) *Watering*

Correct watering has more to do with success in growing succulents than does any other factor. While it is true that these plants can exist for quite lengthy periods without water, during the growing period most of them benefit by being kept well supplied. At this point I am considering only those species whose growing period is in summer. Others will have special directions given later in the book, in Chapter 10. In that chapter, 'plenty of water' means water whenever the soil appears dry; 'moderate watering' means leave for a few days, depending on the weather, before rewatering; while 'exercise care in watering' means that water is given only occasionally when the plant shows signs of shrivelling.

People with only a small number of plants will obtain the best results by immersing the pots in a bowl of tepid water to within half an inch of the rim and leaving them until the surface of the soil appears moist. No further watering is needed until the compost has dried (the pot will give a hollow ring when it is tapped). With a large collection this method takes too long and overhead watering has to be carried out. A good soaking should be given, and with correct drainage and suitable compost excess water quickly drains away. If any water remains on the surface the plant should be repotted with more attention to drainage. During hot, dry weather plants in small pots may need watering every day. Under these conditions a spray in the evening to simulate the dew to which many of them are accustomed in nature is beneficial. At other times it is best to water early in the morning before the sun is on the plants.

In October, watering should be carried out less frequently, say once a week. Intervals between waterings should be lengthened as winter approaches, and during December, January, and February no water need be given to plants kept in a cool greenhouse. (For plants kept in a warm place, see page 33.) The withholding of water is essential when a minimum temperature of about 5°C. (or 40°F.) is aimed at, as perfectly dry plants which are dormant can withstand cold better than those kept growing.

Towards the end of February watering can be restarted on a mild day. A small amount only should be given as during the resting period most of the root hairs will have dried up and the plants are incapable of absorbing much water. From then on the amount and frequency of the watering can be gradually increased until by early May summer watering can be resumed.

If seedlings can be kept at a temperature of above 10°C. (50°F.) during winter by using a specially heated propagating box, it is beneficial for them to be kept growing all winter. In this case the soil should be kept just moist so that the root hairs do not wither away. If these very small plants are dried out completely they suffer a check, because when watering begins in the spring new roots have to form before growth can restart. Sizeable plants can be obtained much more rapidly by this method. A corner of the greenhouse can be used as a propagating box by using boards for the sides and sheets of glass on top. Extra heat is provided by an electric soil cable.

Forest cacti such as *Epiphyllums*, *Rhipsalis*, and *Zygocactus* are not dried out completely in their natural habitats. They should therefore be watered about once a fortnight during the winter and given abundant water when buds begin to show in spring. When flowering is over a resting period is beneficial. So for about six weeks little water should be given but, to prevent shrivelling of the branches, a spray can be given in the evenings of hot days.

Caudiciform *Othonnas*, *Pelargoniums*, *Sarcocaulons*, deciduous *Cotyledons*, *Greenovias*, and many *Mesembryanthemums* are dormant in summer. During that time they should be kept dry, watering being restarted when the plant shows signs of growth such as the formation of leaves, the opening of the previously closed rosettes or other unmistakable signs. Discontinue watering when the leaves wither or the rosettes close. For further details see under the descriptions of the various genera (Chapter 10).

The great point as far as watering is concerned is to make sure that the compost in any pot is not constantly wet. Allow it to dry between watering. Continually wet soil becomes sour and may lead to root rot, or possibly stem rot at the surface of the soil. If pots are stood in saucers make sure that the saucers do not always contain water. In particular make sure that the greenhouse does not leak, as any plant standing under a drip is almost certain to become a casualty. Plants in plastic pots need less water than those in clay pots as there is no loss through the sides. I personally do not favour plastic pots as it is not possible to see when watering is needed.

Plants grown in a warm room, especially one which is centrally heated, need special consideration. The air in such cases is very dry, and the plants will shrivel if no water is given during the winter. About once a fortnight during the winter months they should be watered sufficiently to moisten the soil, but during cold spells must be kept away from the windows after watering.

(E) *Temperature*

At one time most succulents were treated as stove plants, but it is now realized that these plants can withstand very much lower temperatures. Some species of cacti, such as *Lobivias*, *Opuntias*, and so on, grow right up to the snow-line in the Andes, whilst many more can withstand short periods of freezing as long as they are perfectly dry. Few of them, with the exception of *Sempervivums* and some *Sedums*, can survive both cold and damp.

It will be found that a winter temperature that does not fall below about 5° C. (40° F.) will satisfy most of the plants normally seen in small collections. Plants from Central and East Africa and Madagascar, which need up to 60° F., are exceptions. These include the popular *Euphorbia milii* (synonym *E. splendens*), *Adeniums*, and a number of other desirable species. Amongst cacti the interesting *Melocactus* from the West Indies is difficult to winter, and species of *Lemaireocereus* are often lost. To accommodate these some growers fit up a kind of greenhouse within a greenhouse to economize on fuel. Inside this enclosure an attempt is made to maintain a temperature of about 16° C. (60° F.).

Too high a temperature in winter is not good for many species as it keeps them growing all the time and they miss their normal resting period. This interference with their normal rhythm of growth may upset the flowering of the plants. Moreover, maintaining a constant temperature of 10° C. (50° F.) is twice as expensive as to do so for 5° C. (40° F.).

Plants grown in windows need special consideration when the rooms are not centrally heated. During the daytime the room may well be at a temperature of 21° C. (70° F.) or higher. In the early hours of a winter morning, when the windows are covered with frost pictures, the temperature may well fall nearly to freezing-point. This wide variation in daily temperature need not cause too much concern as many plants experience similar conditions in the wild. In the desert of Baluchistan I used to wake to see the rocks covered with hoar-frost whilst in the afternoon the temperature was over 38° C. (100° F.). Provided only the more common species are grown no difficulties should be met with. Rare and expensive plants, however, should not be grown in these conditions.

If plants growing in the house have to be left in an unheated room for some time in the winter, they can be covered by a few sheets of newspaper which will give considerable protection against dry cold. At other times it is sufficient to draw the curtains between the plants and the window. These methods proved adequate here during the very cold spell at the end of 1961.

(F) *Light*

It should be remembered that the intensity of the light in the natural habitats of succulents is far greater than in this country. Thus most of them can take all the sunlight available without coming to any harm. Even so, some very successful growers apply a coating of 'summer cloud' (obtainable, with instructions, from florists' shops) to their greenhouses during the height of summer. (This provides a thin coating of white on the glass which moderates the intensity of the light.) It should be washed off on the approach of autumn and is totally unnecessary in many industrial areas where there is considerable atmospheric pollution. There the glass must be kept washed to get the full benefit of what sun there is.

It has already been mentioned that some species grow in the shade of desert bushes. These will appreciate semi-shade even in this country. In greenhouses where the glass comes down to the ground they can profitably be grown under the staging. Most *Haworthias* and all the *Stapeliads* can be treated in this way. Amongst desert cacti the *Rebutias* and allied genera which grow among dry grass may be scorched if exposed to too much sun, and a position in half-shade is best for them.

Naturally all the forest cacti can be grown in shade. Some magnificent specimens of *Epiphyllum* and *Zygocactus* are to be seen in the north-facing windows of country cottages.

(G) *Ventilation*

Good ventilation is essential, although draughts must be avoided. A close, damp atmosphere encourages the growth of fungi and their spread by means of spores. In summer the ventilators of greenhouses should be open as much as possible, and even in winter they should be open whenever the weather is fine, provided it is not too cold or windy.

3 · Protection

Whilst many succulents enjoy being in the open during the summer, very few are hardy enough to remain outside during our wet winters. Some kind of protection is essential for most of them, but actual outdoor culture is dealt with in Chapter 7.

(A) *Windows*

Most people who start with a few succulents in pots accommodate them in the windows of the house or flat. On the Continent it is by no means uncommon to see all the windows of large blocks of flats crowded with succulents. They are also much in favour as decorations in hotels. The dry warmth of these centrally heated buildings can be tolerated better by succulents than by most other kinds of house plants. But in these circumstances it must be borne in mind that some water must be given at all seasons.

The forest cacti already mentioned can be stood in the north- and east-facing windows, but others, and desert cacti in particular, require the sunniest windows possible. If grown in shade they lose their natural brilliant colours, the spines become weak, and the whole plant becomes elongated and misshapen. Flowers are unlikely to be formed under these conditions.

Enthusiastic growers sometimes fit up sets of shelves in suitable windows and in this way are able to accommodate quite a large number of species, especially if only small-growing plants, suitable for pots up to $3\frac{1}{2}$ inches in diameter, are grown, for example *Rebutias, Mammillarias, Notocacti, Parodias, Crassulas, Adromiscus, Echeverias,* and others which can be chosen from the species given in the second part of the book.

(B) *Greenhouses*

Once the nucleus of a good collection has been grown in the house the need is usually felt for more accommodation, and a greenhouse becomes essential. There are many types of portable greenhouses on the market at reasonable prices for those who cannot afford brick-based structures. When you are deciding which to

9. Exhibit of succulents staged by the Royal Botanic Gardens, Kew

buy, always remember that you get what you pay for, and the very cheap models will tend to develop defects quite soon. Very small houses are not advisable as they cost more to heat in proportion to their size than larger ones do and, in my experience, however large the house is, it will never be large enough to accommodate all the plants you wish to grow. A suitable size for the average collector is 9 feet by 12 or 15 feet. A house of this size can be bought for £50, but small houses can be obtained for £25.

There is a choice of wood or metal frames. Both have advantages and disadvantages. Aluminium houses never rot, they don't need painting, and, as the girders and rafters are much thinner than wooden ones, they let in much more light. On the debit side they are colder owing to conduction by the metal; the glass is not fixed in so firmly and may be blown out, and it is more difficult to fix up shelves and stages.

Wooden ones may be obtained in deal, oak, and red cedar. I have tried them all, and my choice would be a well-constructed house of red cedar. The initial cost may be slightly higher, but this is soon saved on maintenance: one big advantage is that red cedar doesn't need painting.

Both metal and wooden houses in which the glass reaches down to the ground are available. They need more fuel to maintain a given temperature than those which are boarded to the level of the stages, but the space under the stages can be used for many kinds of plants so that the growing area is nearly double, and on the whole I think I prefer this type.

Wooden staging needs replacing every few years. I have found asbestos sheets carried by strong supports very suitable. On the asbestos a layer of sand on which the pots rest can be placed, and this, of course, will last indefinitely. Another permanent arrangement is the use of aluminium trays or deep boxes in which a plunge bed can be made using sand or sifted, well-weathered furnace ash. In this the smaller-sized pots are plunged. This prevents them drying out too quickly in hot weather and saves much watering.

Heating may be by coke, paraffin, or electricity. If a high winter temperature is desired a system of a boiler, using coke, and hot-water pipes is the most economical. The attention that it needs is its chief drawback, particularly late on a cold winter's night. There is also the expense of installation.

A good paraffin stove is convenient when the electricity supply is too distant, but it should be one that gives a blue flame, as in this type fumes are reduced to a minimum. Many gardeners, particularly those who grow plants with delicate foliage, dislike oil stoves. Poor-quality stoves leave some of the paraffin unburnt. The resulting fumes enter the leaves by way of the stomata and poison the leaf. Even first-rate stoves produce enough fumes to damage those plants with numerous stomata. In the case of succulents there are relatively few stomata and so, in most cases, oil stoves can be used with perfectly satisfactory results. I have a large house heated in this way and have never noted any damage except that leafy *Cotyledons* have dropped a few leaves.

The stove should be large enough to ensure a minimum temperature of 5°C. (40°F.) even during very cold spells. Beware of stoves advertised as using only very small amounts of paraffin. A gallon of paraffin, if burnt completely as happens with an efficient blue-flame stove, gives only a certain number of calories, whatever the type of stove.

10. Cacti in the Sherman Hoyt House at Kew. This was originally a reproduction of part of Death Valley in the U.S.A., but in natural conditions the plants are far more widely separated

Heating by means of electricity is the least troublesome, but the most expensive, method. If the system is fitted with a thermostat it can be switched on and left for the winter, with the knowledge that there will be no waste, as once the temperature rises above that desired the current will automatically be switched off. Of course, the temperature should be checked daily in case a fault has developed in the wiring. When deciding on the temperature at which to set the thermostat, bear in mind that every extra 3°C. (5°F.) or so over 7°C. (45°F.) doubles the cost.

Electrical heating can be carried out by tubular heaters, stoves, fan heaters, convector heaters, or cables. Fan heaters are the most satisfactory and cost from £9 upwards. Again, I should stress that whichever is used should have sufficient power to maintain the temperature during very cold spells. You can find out from an electricity showroom the number of kilowatts needed for your particular greenhouse.

If you decide to use electricity to heat your greenhouse, it is helpful to fit up part of one stage as a propagating frame, using soil-heating cables to give the extra heat needed.

11. Group of *Mammillarias* showing the very diverse nature of this large but very popular genus

Many growers advocate the use of polythene sheets fastened on the inside of the greenhouse so that there is a gap between the polythene and glass. This makes use of the same principle as the cavity walls of houses. I have heard it claimed that in a fully covered greenhouse a saving of about 3°C. (5°F.) is made. A disadvantage is the condensation with consequent drip, so watch out for this. There is also loss of light intensity, though this probably does not matter so much in winter as most of the plants will be dormant.

(c) *Frames*

Many of the hardier succulents can be wintered in a deep brick-built frame, covered by mats during cold spells. Whenever weather conditions allow, the lights should be raised to provide the necessary fresh air.

I have also seen excellent results obtained for the cultivation of dwarf succulents by the use of low frames filled nearly to the top with a suitable compost and heated by electrical heating strips fitted round the sides.

4 · Propagation

Whilst many of the commoner succulents can be easily and rapidly propagated by means of various parts of the plant, most cacti and the rarer succulents need to be raised from seeds. It is possible to obtain collected plants of the slow-growing species, but they are expensive. Moreover, unless they are bought well rooted from a nursery they are not easy to establish. Watering of such plants must be carried out with extreme care, the pots being kept practically dry until new roots are formed, which may take some months. A light syringing occasionally helps to prevent withering.

(A) *Seeds*

Raising cacti from seeds is not difficult provided certain rules are followed, and a collection of such plants can give far more satisfaction than the same plants bought 'ready-made'. The most important necessity is warmth. A soil temperature of about 16 to 21°C. (60 to 70°F.) is essential for germination. This means that a seed propagator must be used or else the seeds should not be sown until late May or June. In the latter case the young plants will be very small during their first winter and there may be some losses. I have seen it suggested that the seed pan should be placed in the airing-cupboard for warmth, but I would not recommend this. Unless taken into the light as soon as germination has taken place the young plants become spindly and weak and soon die. Removed from the warmth to a lower temperature they suffer a severe check. It is still worse if mixed seeds are sown as they germinate at different rates, so that whilst some need taking out of the cupboard, others still need the warmth. There are a number of cheap electrically heated seed propagators on the market, costing from 30s upwards. A good type has a heating element embedded in a plastic sheet which slides underneath the seed box. It is also possible to improvise one. A wooden box deep enough to take a 15-watt bulb is needed. Over this place a piece of

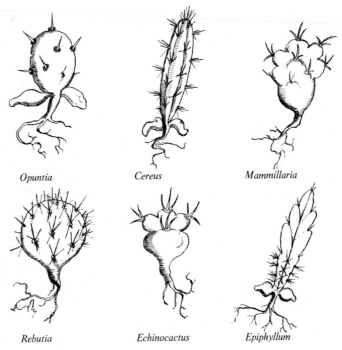

| *Opuntia* | *Cereus* | *Mammillaria* |
| *Rebutia* | *Echinocactus* | *Epiphyllum* |

Fig. 1. Types of seedlings of cacti

sheet-iron, and then a shallow seed box. Cover the box with glass to keep in the warmth.

A very open, sterilized soil mixture should be used. I advise using John Innes Compost Number 1. The seed box can be divided into compartments by wooden or metal strips, and the soil given a soaking. Very small seeds should not be covered; larger ones like *Opuntias* and *Cerei* should be pressed into the soil before covering.

The glass should be turned and wiped at intervals to prevent any drips. If rain-water is used for watering it should be boiled to kill spores of moss and algae, and then allowed to cool. The soil must never be allowed to dry, but on the other hand should not be kept water-logged. Watering must be done with a very fine rose

12. Pans of year-old seedlings. The three pans in the foreground are *Euphorbias*, showing their close resemblance to cacti

on the can, or the seeds may be washed to the side of the container. Most cacti seeds will germinate in a few days, but some *Opuntias* and related genera may take much longer, even exceeding a year.

Opuntias have seed leaves like ordinary plants, *Cerei* have rudimentary seed leaves, but the globular cacti have none and first show as tiny green balls which may need a magnifying glass to see. The *Opuntias* and *Cerei* grow fairly rapidly, but the others are slow and should remain undisturbed until the following spring when they can be pricked out in boxes or into individual small pots. By forcing it is possible to have them big enough to prick out in their first season, but softly grown plants lack good spine formation and are more easily lost by fungus infection.

43

For the reasons given I do not advocate the sowing of mixed seeds, but by sowing a dozen packets of named seeds each year a good collection can soon be built up at small cost. *Rebutias* and some *Mammillarias* will flower two years after seed sowing; *Parodias*, *Astrophytums*, *Notocacti*, and others after three years; while many *Cerei*, *Ferocacti*, and such-like will not bloom in a dozen years. The time taken to reach flowering size naturally depends on the cultural methods adopted. I have seen *Epiphyllums* in flower three years to the day from seed sowing, although the time taken is usually considerably longer. The secret in this case was a high winter temperature with continuous watering all the year round. It is necessary to balance the cost of such treatment with the desirability of rapid growth of the seedlings.

Most of the other succulents are easier and quicker than cacti. Many of the *Mesembryanthemums*, for example, will flower in their first year.

(B) *Offsets*

Many succulents such as *Agaves*, *Aloes*, *Gasterias*, *Haworthias*, *Sempervivums*, and *Sedums* produce many young plants round the base of the old plant, each with its own roots, and these can be dug out, potted, and treated like the parent plant.

(C) *Cuttings*

Those succulents that form clusters or branching shrubs can have suitable pieces cut off for use as cuttings. The shrubby *Crassulas*, some *Euphorbias*, *Stapelias*, *Echeverias*, *Cotyledons*, and *Opuntias*, among others, may be treated in this way. Some of the cacti, such as *Echinopsis*, *Trichocereus*, *Rebutias*, *Lobivias*, and some *Mammillarias*, form unrooted offsets either round the base or higher up. These, likewise, can be cut off and used as cuttings. Certain *Aeoniums*, *Echeverias*, and *Pachyphytums* grow leggy after a time, and in these cases the top should be cut off and used as a cutting. The stump will produce a large number of small rosettes which, when large enough, can also be taken as cuttings. Some of the *Cerei* may become too tall for their position. These can likewise be beheaded and the top rooted, whilst the cut part will send out shoots suitable for cuttings. Other lower-growing cacti, such as

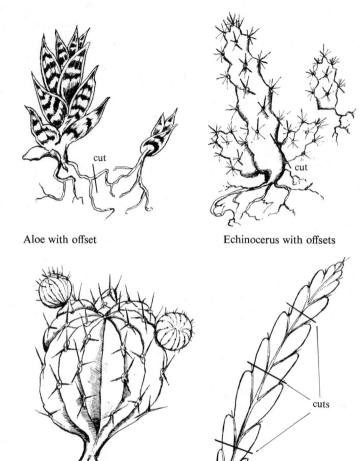

Aloe with offset

Echinocerus with offsets

Echinopsis with offsets

Flat stem of epiphyllum cut
to produce 3 cuttings

Fig. 2. Propagation from offsets and by cutting up a flat stem

45

13. Propagating bed with cuttings

columnar *Mammillarias*, can also be induced to provide suitable shoots by having their tops cut off, but this is only to be recommended if seeds are unobtainable.

When taking cuttings a very sharp knife should be used. Before being planted in a very sandy mixture they should be dried for some days until the cut surface has calloused, and little water should be given after they have been planted until they have rooted. Some growers use vermiculite as a rooting medium, but as this contains no nutriment, the plants need potting as soon as they are well rooted.

(D) *Leaf Cuttings*

Most members of the very large family *Crassulaceae* can be propagated by leaf cuttings. If a well-grown leaf of a *Crassula*, *Pachyphytum*, or some *Echeverias* or *Sedums*, is carefully detached so as not to injure it and then laid on sandy soil, a small plant will be produced from the point of detachment. As the young plant grows so the leaf withers away. When large enough the plantlets can be potted and treated as mature plants.

The larger leaves of *Gasterias* and some *Aloes* should be partly buried at the lower end and a cluster of plantlets will then be formed there. Leaves of the *Mesembryanthemum* family will sometimes form roots, but as no shoot is produced this method of propagation will not work for this family.

Rooted leaf cutting of *Gasteria* showing plantlets

Rooted leaf cutting of *Adromischus* showing plantlets

Fig. 3. Leaf cuttings

(E) *Plantlets*

Bryophyllums form round their leaves tiny plantlets which sometimes grow roots whilst still attached to the leaves (Pl. 14); others fall off and root where they drop. As a single plant can form hundreds of these plantlets they can become something of a nuisance and may have to be weeded out of the pots of other plants. Other species of *Bryophyllum* develop plantlets from adventitious buds (Pl. 15). *Agaves* and *Fourcraeas* form bulbils in the axils of the inflorescence which can be used for propagation. *Crassula multicava*, likewise, forms plantlets amongst the flowers.

(F) *Grafting*

Grafting is extensively practised by continental growers, but is not so popular in this country, as in many cases the resulting plant looks like a drumstick. The practice is useful in that slow-growing

14. Leaf of *Bryophyllum crenatum* showing how the plantlets start growing while still attached to the leaves

15. Adventitious buds on *Bryophyllum tubiflorum*

16. *Matucana hystrix* grafted on a *Cereus*. This leads to more rapid growth but a drumstick appearance

plants can be more rapidly brought to flowering size; plants that are difficult to grow on their own roots are preserved; abnormal forms such as crests can be propagated; small bits of plants nearly lost by rotting can be saved; and trailing plants such as *Aporocactus* can be grown as standards and so improve their display. A disadvantage is that the more rapid growth is detrimental to spine formation, and grafted plants are seldom true to the wild types.

It should be emphasized that stock and scion should belong to the same family. It is useless, for example, to try to graft a cactus on a *Kleinia*, as I once saw being done. The usual stocks for cacti are *Pereskia*, *Opuntia* (not recommended), and the commoner *Cerei*.

Both stock and scion should be in vigorous growth, and for best results the sizes of the two cut surfaces should be the same. The cuts are best made with a razor blade. The top is removed from the stock and can usually be used as a cutting. The top part

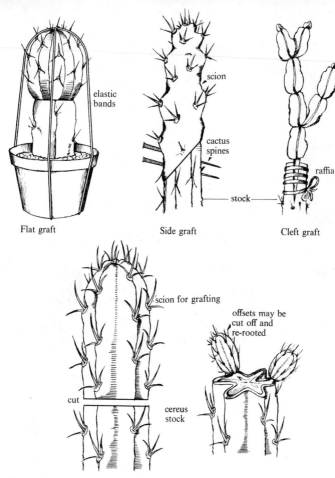

Fig. 4. Types of grafts

of the scion is then cut off and immediately, before any drying can take place, is placed on top of the stock and the two cut surfaces pressed together. Rubber bands passed over the top of the scion and under the pot will keep the surfaces in contact until union occurs. After grafting keep the new plant warm and shaded. The stock should be watered, but no water should be allowed to reach the union.

5 · Pests and diseases

(A) *Mealy Bugs*

These are sucking insects, similar to greenfly, that cover themselves with a protective coating of wax which looks like cotton wool. They can be very troublesome when they get between the leaf bases of such plants as *Aeoniums* and *Faucarias*, and, as they are inclined to multiply most on the side of the plant away from the gangway, an occasional all-round examination of plants should be made. When the infestation is not bad the pests can be painted over with methylated spirit to which two-and-a-half per cent nicotine has been added; the alcohol dissolves the waxy protection. Spraying with malathion is very effective, though this chemical must not be used on members of the *Crassulaceae*. The use of a petroleum emulsion spray, such as Volck, will kill the bugs but will also dissolve the waxy 'bloom' that is one of the beauties of many succulents.

(B) *Root Mealy Bugs*

This is a similar pest that attacks the roots of plants, and it is favoured by dry conditions. Its presence is not suspected until a plant begins to look unhealthy. If the white wool is seen on the roots all soil should be shaken off and the roots dipped in methylated spirit containing nicotine. Allow the roots to dry before repotting in fresh soil. Crystals of paradichlorobenzene (obtainable from any chemist) in the bottom of the pot will keep the pest at bay.

(C) *Scale Insects*

These sucking insects protect themselves with a covering shield which guards them from most insecticides. Hand picking, using blunt tweezers, is the only reliable remedy. In bad cases of infestation the scales may be brushed off with a stiff toothbrush and the plants given an oil emulsion spray.

 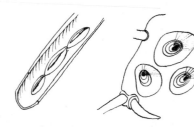

(a) Mealy bug

(b) Scale insect
on *Yucca*

(c) Scale insect
on *Euphorbia*

Fig. 5. Mealy bug and scale insects
(all greatly enlarged)

(D) *Red Spider*

These greenhouse pests are very tiny and you may need a magnifying glass to see them, but the appearance of rusty-looking patches at the top of a plant indicates their presence. They are particularly likely to attack cacti as they thrive in a dry atmosphere. They are discouraged by frequent syringing with water, but when established are best dealt with by fumigating with Azobenzene cones. D.D.T. sprays are also effective.

(E) *Aphids*

These blackfly or greenfly, similar to those found on beans and roses, are especially troublesome on the flowers of both cacti and other succulents. Any proprietary insecticide spray will easily deal with them. Besides the direct damage they do, they also excrete a sticky fluid which falls on the rest of the plant and produces black incrustations very difficult to remove.

(F) *Ants*

While these insects do no direct damage they are responsible for carrying the pests mentioned above from plant to plant. If they are observed in the house, one of the proprietary ant killers should be used.

(G) *Stem Rot*

Incorrect watering, the use of too much nitrogenous fertilizer, or other defects of cultivation, may lead to fungus attacks which cause rotting, usually just above the soil. In this case the top of the plant must be cut off and treated as a cutting. The fungus spreads inside the plant tissues and causes a reddish-brown stain. When making the cutting it must be cut back to a point where no sign of this discoloration is apparent. If, when this has been done, only a small piece of healthy shoot is left, then it is best to graft it.

If soft spots develop on other parts of a cactus, the diseased material should be scraped out and the cut surface treated with flowers of sulphur and allowed to dry. No water should be given until the injury is healed.

(H) *Root Rot*

If a plant fails to grow, examination may reveal that the roots have rotted, probably because of bad drainage. All diseased roots should be cut back to a point where the flesh is quite white, the cuts treated with sulphur, and the plant left to dry. It can then be treated as a cutting.

6 · Bowl gardens and floral arrangements

Bowl gardens can make attractive decorations for rooms, particularly in winter. A neutral-coloured, plain bowl which will not clash with the colours of the plants is best. A reasonably deep container should be used, at least three inches deep, to allow for drainage and a sufficiently deep root run. A bowl without drainage holes will ensure that the furniture is not damaged by water, and for the same reason glazed pottery is preferable. I have seen such bowl gardens remain in excellent condition for a couple of years until the plants became too large for the bowl (Pls. 17–20).

Where there are no drainage holes, it is essential to use plenty of drainage material in the bottom of the bowl. Broken crocks are best – large pieces at the base, covered by smaller material to a depth of an inch. Amongst the crocks should be mixed pieces of charcoal to keep the soil from becoming sour. The bowl is then filled with a fairly rich but open compost.

Some growers dislike mixing cacti and other succulents in the same bowl, partly because of their different habitats, but mainly because the spiny cacti do not harmonize with the smooth, rounded leaves of most of the other succulents. However, this is a matter of personal opinion and from the point of view of cultivation there is no reason why they should not be mixed. Easy, relatively slow-growing species should be chosen. There are plenty of very decorative plants available for use, which are easy to propagate and which look just as well as more expensive rarities. The latter are liable to be damaged, or even lost, in the less natural conditions of the bowl garden.

Suitable cacti for an all-cactus bowl are *Opuntia microdasys*, all species of *Rebutia*, cluster-forming *Mammillarias* such as *prolifera*, *gracilis*, *bocasana* and *elongata*, *Chamaecereus sylvestris*, *Echinopsis* offsets, and young plants of any of the columnar *Cerei* to give height.

Amongst other succulents the following can be recommended:

17. Bowl garden planted with quick-growing succulents. This will need replanting very shortly

18. Bowl garden planted mainly with cacti. These do not lend themselves so easily to the art of the flower arranger

19. Bowl garden planted with cacti and other succulents, allowing room for growth

20. A bowl of succulents showing how they can be used by the flower arranger. They are too close for a permanent planting

Crassula tetragona and *C. lycopodioides*, *Kleinia articulata*, *Sedum treleasei*, *S. pachyphyllum*, and *S. adolfii* for height; *Haworthia fasciata* and *H. attenuata*, *Aloe aristata*, *Dudleya farinosa*, *Echeveria secunda*, *E. setosa*, *E. derenbergii*, and *E. glauca* as intermediates, with *Crassula cooperi*, *C. socialis*, and *C. nealeana*, *Sedum stahlii* and *S. rubrotinctum*, *Oscularia deltoides* and *Delosperma echinatum* in the foreground. A selection of these would give an arrangement as colourful as an arrangement of flowers. Do not use *Lithops*, *Conophytums*, or other stemless *Mesembryanthemums* as they are unsuited to bowl culture. Do not crowd the plants.

By the use of selected pieces of rock the plants can be shown up better. With a large bowl a landscape effect can be produced. When the planting is finished a top dressing of stone chips, pea gravel, or coarse sand should be given.

The bowl should be kept in the sunniest place available. If kept away from a window it should be removed to the greenhouse from time to time to allow the plants to recover from the lack of sunlight.

The plants must be watered with care because of the absence of drainage holes. Water until the soil is saturated and then allow it to dry out before giving more water. During winter, if the bowl is in a heated room, watering as above will probably be required once every two weeks; if the room is cold, once a month should be sufficient, and then only if there is no frost. In summer more water is needed, according to conditions.

It will probably be necessary to replant the bowl every year, as some of the plants will grow out of proportion to the others.

In floral arrangements use is frequently made of foliage. Those enthusiasts with reasonably large collections of succulents will find that prunings from their larger specimens are admirable for use in some unusual designs. Rosettes of various *Aeoniums* and *Echeverias*, branches of the larger-growing *Cotyledons*, *Pachyphytums*, and *Sedums*, and flowering stems of *Rhipsalis* and some *Ceropegias* can all be used. Green, blue, red, yellowish, bronze, and variegated foliage can all be obtained in this way and provide colours that are unobtainable from flowers alone.

7 · Succulents in the open

In South Africa and California succulents are often used for furnishing rock gardens, where they look very much at home. But in only the mildest parts of this country, such as the Scilly Isles and near the coast of Cornwall, can most of them be used in this way. However, there are some perfectly hardy varieties and others that are reasonably hardy which are very useful additions to the rock garden in all parts of the country. All *Sempervivums* grow well in the joints between rocks, and by filling the cracks help to give the impression that one large rock, instead of several smaller ones, has been used. The dwarf *Sedums* can be used on hot, dry banks where little else will flourish, and by a suitable choice of varieties a multi-coloured carpet can soon be obtained. Suitable species are *S. acre* with its golden and white variegated forms, *S. album* var. *chloroticum* (pale green), *S. album* var. *murale* (purplish), *S. anglicum* (reddish), *S. brevifolium* (white), *S. dasyphyllum* (bluish), *S. hispanicum* (grey-green), and *S. oreganum* (cherry red). *Sedums* suitable for trailing over rocks are *S. caulicolon* and *S. sieboldii* with pink flowers in autumn, and *S. kamtschaticum* with deep yellow flowers in summer. *S. spectabile* is suitable either for the large rockery or herbaceous border, growing upwards of a foot high and having large heads of bright pink flowers in August. *Rosularias* and *Orostachys* may survive if the winters are not too severe.

Agave parryi will grow outside in a hot place, facing south with a large rock behind it to reflect the warmth. Some low-growing *Opuntias*, such as *O. polyacantha*, *O. greenii*, *O. brachyarthra*, and others, will likewise survive on a well-drained, sunny bank.

Another way of using succulents in the open is to treat them as summer bedding plants. Many of the shrubby *Mesembryanthemums* will do well on dry, stony slopes. Recommended are species of *Lampranthus*, *Oscularia*, *Delosperma*, *Drosanthemum*, and *Ruschia*, all of which form large mats and cover themselves with brightly coloured flowers, daisy-like in appearance but botanically quite different. It is best to take cuttings of these in August

21. *Dorotheanthus criniflorus*, an annual mesembryanthemum, used for summer bedding. This is more often found in seed lists under the name *Mesembryanthemum criniflorum*

and not to attempt to save the old plants. With them may be grown the annuals *Dorotheanthus criniflorus* (Pl. 21) and *Cryophytum crystallinum*. Some excellent examples of this can be seen in the public parks and promenades of many summer resorts.

The larger-growing *Opuntias*, *Cerei*, *Aloes*, *Agaves*, and *Crassulas* appreciate open-air treatment in the summer. They should not be removed from their pots, but if you wish to make a bed of them, as is often done on the Continent, the pots should be buried so as not to destroy the illusion of plants growing naturally.

Really tropical effects can be obtained by the use of these and other genera that grow rather too large for the average-sized greenhouse before they develop their true character, genera such as *Dasylirions*, *Beschornerias*, *Nolinas*, *Fourcraeas*, and *Puyas*.

22. Succulents bedded out at Kew. Note the flower bud on the relatively small *Agave* to the right of the planting. The tall plants are partly *Cerei* and partly *Euphorbias*

This is practised at Kew Gardens as is well shown in Pl. 22. Other excellent examples can be found in some provincial public parks such as at Kettering (Northants), although there cacti are kept in beds separate from the other succulents. This method of growing large specimens is carried out by some private growers who lack greenhouse space. During winter the plants are kept under greenhouse stages, in spare bedrooms, in reasonably frost-proof sheds, or even in the attics of the house.

Very large specimens of *Agaves* can be grown in tubs to ornament verandas or terraces. In winter they should be covered with straw and sacks or moved into a shed.

Young plants and small-growing species should not be exposed to the rigours of an English summer.

8 · Showing

Added interest can be given to succulent growing by entering your plants at shows. Shows devoted exclusively to succulents are organized by cactus societies in many parts of the country, and many horticultural societies include a number of classes for succulents. Just visiting these shows is very helpful, both in giving you a chance to see what well-grown plants should look like and in encouraging you to improve your own standard of cultivation.

Before showing, study the instructions for judges drawn up by the R.H.S. in consultation with the show committees of the cactus societies. Briefly, these instructions lay down that forty per cent of the points should be awarded for cultivation, twenty per cent for rarity, twenty per cent for difficulty, and twenty per cent for trueness to type, that is, what the plant looks like in its natural habitat.

Before taking plants to a show make sure that they (and their pots) are clean, and in particular that they are free from insect pests. Neat labels with correct names are helpful. Plants in flower, bud, or fruit have an advantage over others. In classes for more than one plant as great a variety as possible should be aimed at, e.g. in a class for three cacti don't show three *Mammillarias* but plants of three distinct genera, whilst in a class for three *Mammillarias* choose plants that are as different as possible from each other.

Before deciding on which plants to enter, read the schedule carefully to make sure your plants conform to it. Failure to do this may lead to disqualification. Pots even a fraction of an inch above the stated size are no good. If there is any doubt about the eligibility of any plant the show secretary should be consulted.

If you are disappointed by the judge's decision, take note of the plant he considers better than yours and decide to improve on your performance at the next show.

23. A Chelsea Show exhibit of mature plants,
some in flower, mainly cacti

9 · Nomenclature and classification

Many people find it difficult to learn the Latin names of succulent plants and ask for their common names. Actually, as all these plants are exotics most of them have no common names in this country. Attempts by some American nurserymen to popularize these plants by inventing common names have led to such absurdities as 'Baby's Toes' and 'Baby's Breath'. Gardeners accept such botanical names as *Chrysanthemum*, *Gladiolus*, *Dahlia*, and *Fuchsia* without question, so why not *Mammillaria*, *Ferocactus*, and *Zygocactus*? Common names of plants can be misleading as the same plant may be given different names in various parts of its habitat, whilst the same common name may be given to entirely different plants. *Echinopsis multiplex* is called the 'White Easter Lily' in the United States, but (a) it is not a lily, (b) in this country it doesn't flower at Easter, and (c) there are a number of other *Echinopsis* with white flowers in cultivation. The 'Strawberry Hedgehog' of the U.S.A. is *Echinocereus engelmannii*, whilst the 'Chartreuse Hedgehog' is *Echinomastus johnsonii*, quite different both in shape and flower. At the same time there are quite a number of *Echinocerei* with strawberry-coloured flowers. These instances could be multiplied, so it can easily be seen that the use of common names is most misleading.

The botanical names of plants are in two parts: first the genus, then the species. Plants in the same genus usually closely resemble each other; if not, the structure of the flowers is the same. The specific name serves to distinguish plants in the same genus. There may be a third varietal name when the difference is not sufficiently marked for the plant to be a new species. Thus the genus *Mammillaria* consists of plants where the body is covered with nipples, *M. plumosa* is a species where each nipple is tipped with a feather-like tuft of hairs, *M. microcarpa* is covered with hooked spines, whilst *M. rhodantha* forms a spiny column with varieties *sulphurea* (pale yellow spines), *rubra* (red spines), *fuscata* (brown-tipped yellow spines), and so on.

24. Cristate cacti
Back row: *Opuntia cylindrica, Parodia microsperma, Cephalocereus chrysacanthus*
Front row: *Mammillaria magnimamma, Mammillaria wildii*

Related genera are grouped into families, the relationship being based solely on flower structure. Thus we find some succulents in families consisting mainly of non-succulent plants, although the cactus family consists entirely of succulents. Family names end in the suffix '*aceae*', for example, *Cactaceae*. Besides the *Cactaceae* the most important families containing succulents are the *Agavaceae*, the *Asclepiadaceae*, which includes all the *Stapeliads* and others, the *Compositae* or Daisy family, the *Crassulaceae*, the *Euphorbiaceae*, the *Liliaceae*, the *Mesembryanthemaceae*, and the *Portulacaceae*. All these contain many well-known succulents. Thirty-four other families contain a few succulent members, but as they are not often seen they can be omitted from this short account.

25. *Echinopsis
multiplex cristata*

The *Cactaceae* is such a large family that for convenience it has been subdivided into tribes and sub-tribes. Botanists are still undecided about the relationship between the different plants, and there are for this reason several systems of classification in use. The one still in most favour was formulated by the American botanists Britton and Rose between 1919 and 1923. Later botanists have renamed many of the plants, and so we find the same plant grown under different names according to which particular botanists are favoured. Thus most growers in this country speak of *Epiphyllums*, although some continental botanists use the older name *Phyllocactus*. Britton and Rose divide the family into three tribes, the *Pereskieae*, leafy plants; the *Opuntieae*, jointed like the Prickly Pear; and the *Cereeae* which, being the largest, is again divided into sub-tribes. It is not necessary here to go into details of these except to note that the *Hylocereanae*, the *Epiphyllanae*, and the *Rhipsalidanae* contain the forest cacti and so will be dealt with separately in the following descriptions of the *Cactaceae*.

In addition to the numerous natural species, collections of succulents often contain what are known as cristate (Pl. 24) and monstrose forms. These may have developed from a branch of an otherwise normal plant whilst occasionally a seedling may take such a shape. In a cristate plant or crest the growing part develops

66

26. *Cereus peruvianus monstrosus*

into a line instead of being concentrated at a point. This produces a flattened stem in place of the normal round one and it may appear something like the comb of a hen. In other cases it forms a series of convolutions that have a great attraction to some people. Both cacti and other succulents form these crests, which are so different from the normal forms that in many cases they can be most difficult to name. Sometimes a shoot may revert to the normal form in which case it should be removed and used as a cutting. Otherwise it spoils the symmetry of the plant which is one of the main charms of a crest. In monstrose plants a number of growing-points are formed on one stem. 'Monstrose' in this case has the same meaning as 'monstrous', i.e. malformed or unnatural. This monstrosity takes various forms. In *Opuntia clavaroides monstrosa*, sometimes called the 'Monkey's Paw', each normally tapering branch becomes club-shaped, whilst *O. tuna monstrosa* takes on the conical shape of a 'Noah's ark' tree with innumerable small cylindrical shoots. In other cases we find an abnormal number of small, malformed shoots, as in *Cereus peruvianus monstrosus* (Pl. 26). As the phenomena are not inherited such plants must be propagated vegetatively, usually by grafting. The origin of these abnormalities is not known.

10 · Description of succulent plants

(A) THE CACTACEAE

In a small book of this nature it is not possible to mention more than a small number of the thousands of species that are known to botanists. It is not even possible to include all the 220 genera that have been described. Of these some are unobtainable in this country, some are rare and costly, whilst others test the skill of the most experienced growers. In some of the larger genera many species are so much alike that most of them can be omitted from the average collection and left to the specialist. Still others, whilst small enough to be grown in an average-sized greenhouse, have so little of interest about them that they are not worth growing.

In general, only those plants have been included that are reasonably easy to obtain, relatively easy to grow, and which form good-looking specimens in pots of not more than five inches in diameter. Even so, many plants well known to many readers will be perforce omitted, and a few plants not conforming to the above will be described if they are of outstanding interest. No species is included that cannot be grown anywhere in the country.

Readers who require full descriptions of the plants should consult *Cacti* by J. Borg, published by Macmillan. The most complete work in English on the subject is *The Cactaceae* by Britton and Rose, published in 1923 in America, but this has long been out of print and does not include, of course, the many discoveries of the last forty years. For those who can read German *Die Cactaceae* by Backeberg, in six volumes, published in 1962, can be recommended, as it brings our knowledge of the subject right up to date, including even plants still waiting to be named.

Beginners are warned against naming plants from photographs as many species, or even genera, bear close resemblances to one another, particularly when young. The best way to become familiar with the plants is to visit public and private collections, attend shows, and, best of all, join a society specializing in succulents.

In the following pages genera are grouped under the tribes and sub-tribes of Britton and Rose, as plants in the same sub-tribe have certain relations to each other, in both appearance and cultural requirements.

Plants marked * are often sold in shops for half-a-crown. Other can be obtained from 2s 6d upwards from specialist nurseries.

Tribe 1. *Pereskieae*

The only genus of importance in this tribe is *Pereskia*.

Pereskias are spiny shrubs with woody stems and fairly large, evergreen leaves. They have no resemblance to the popular conception of a cactus but can be recognized by the large woolly areoles. They flower only when very large but are largely used as grafting stock.

P. aculeata. Branches up to 30 feet long. Flowers large, white, with golden stamens. Can be grown trained on a greenhouse wall.

P. aculeata var. *godseffiana*. Worth growing as a small plant as it has leaves prettily variegated with red (Pl. 27).

Tribe 2. *Opuntieae*

Of the eight genera in this tribe only two, *Opuntia* and *Nopalea*, are of importance to us.

All plants in this tribe possess, in addition to spines, glochids, which are loose tufts of barbed bristles on the areoles which come out easily when touched and embed themselves in the skin. They are too fine to be seen easily, but certainly make themselves felt. Some species, too, have sheathed spines which attach themselves firmly to anyone careless enough to brush against them, so much so that the whole branch is more liable to pull away from the plant than the spines to relax their hold. *Opuntia tunicata*, *O. salmiana*, and *O. imbricata* are particularly noteworthy in this respect. Young growths possess small, awl-shaped leaves which are usually short-lived, although on a few species they are fairly persistent.

Opuntia : This is a very large genus with a range extending from Canada to Patagonia and southern Chile. As it covers such a vast area it is not surprising that the species adopts many forms from large bushes and trees of considerable size to low-growing cushions. To allow for this variation the genus was first divided into four sub-genera and is now divided by some botanists into a number of new genera. As most people still call them all *Opuntias*, this practice will be followed here, but those species described will be arranged according to the sub-genera.

Most species have to be a considerable size before flowering so that growers who want flowers are advised to try other genera. Some are very decorative in form, with brightly coloured spines and thick wool, but others often seen are not worth growing. These include *Opuntia leptocaulis*, *O. kleiniae*, and *O. aurantiaca* which often masquerades as *O. salmiana*, a much better plant. All species are readily propagated by cuttings.

Sub-genus Cylindropuntia : These plants have cylindrical stems and branches, the latter divided into elongated joints.

O. clavarioides. Low bush, greyish-brown in colour with short white hairlike spines flat on pads. Usually seen as a monstrose form, called 'Monkey's Paw'. In this the ends of the joints are swollen, with small projections like fingers. Very slow-growing on its own roots, so it is usually grafted. Best in half-shade. Seldom flowers.

*O. cylindrica. Columnar plant several feet high and 2 inches in diameter. Seldom branches. Grass green with white areoles and spines. Small leaves at top which soon fall. Flowers on old plants, red.

O. pachypus. Habit like a *Cereus*, up to 3 feet high. Large areoles with about thirty whitish spines. Cristate form commoner than type. One of best *Opuntias*.

*O. salmiana. Much branched shrub with thin, cylindrical joints. Many glochids and numerous hooked spines. Flowers freely when young, with pale yellow flowers. Scarlet fruits remain on plant and sprout fresh branches. Old branches often turn scarlet. Very showy.

*O. subulata. Strong growing. Over 6 feet high and well branched. Persistent leaves up to 4 inches long. Strong, long, pale yellow spines. Flowers large and red.

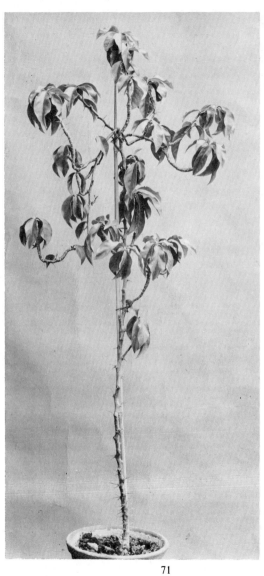

27. *Pereskia aculeata* var. *godseffiana*, a cactus with large leaves

28. *Opuntia*, sub-genus *Tephrocactus*, *platyacantha*

O. tunicata. Erect plant with branches in horizontal whorls. Numerous long, white, sheathed spines make it dangerous to handle.

*O. vestita. Erect, cylindrical stems branching from base. Slender, pliable spines mixed with long white hair. Small leaves persist for a time. Cristate form often seen, with flattened, convolute stems which look as if trimmed with ermine.

Sub-genus Tephrocactus: Low-growing, South American *Opuntias* with oval joints. Spines often flat and papery. Seldom flowers in England.

O. diademata. Usually called *O. papyracantha*. Low-growing, with oval, brownish-green joints. Spines, up to 4 inches long, flat and papery. Slow-growing, needs half-shade.

O. floccosa. Forms mats several yards across entirely hidden in long white hair in the Andes, but hair is very thinly produced in the softer conditions of our greenhouses. Yellow spines hidden by hair.

29. *Opuntia compressa*

O. platyacantha. Prostrate. Joints oval, brownish-green, almost smooth. Spines flat and flexible (Pl. 28).

O. strobiliformis. Erect and much branched. Greyish-green oval pads, with prominent warts and no spines. Pads resemble small pine-cones. Pads fall off if kept too dry.

Sub-genus Platyopuntia : Plants have more or less flattened pads; circular, oval, or cordate. Strong-growing and soon need large pots.

O. arenaria. Pads up to 2 inches long. Areoles brown with long spines. Large pale yellow flowers on relatively small plants.

O. basilaris. Very fleshy, cordate pads; grey-green, often tinged purple in sun. Glochids red-brown, closely set. No spines. Large carmine flowers. Recommended.

O. compressa. Prostrate with thick, oval joints. Spines almost absent. Flowers pale yellow (Pl. 29).

30. *Opuntia gosseliniana*

O. gosseliniana. Almost circular pads, prominent yellow glochids, and long, slender, pliable spines, reddish when young but
turning white with age. Striking species (Pl. 30).

*O. leucotricha. Elongated oval pads with long, stiff, curling
spines resembling hair. Strong, upright growth. Deep yellow
flowers seldom seen.

*O. microdasys. Handsome even as a small plant. No spines,
but areoles very conspicuous with tufts of yellow glochids, easily

31. *Opuntia microdasys*

detached (Pl. 31). *O. m. albispina* has white glochids and *O. rufida* red ones. Pads easily fall if kept too dry.

*O. monacantha. Very quick-growing, with long, oval, shining green joints. Areoles widely separated with single, long, brown spine from each. *O. m. variegata* is smaller, beautifully marbled with white and yellow.

O. santa-rita. Almost circular pads, deep bluish green in colour. Quite spineless but aeroles with prominent tufts of reddish glochids.

O. scheerii. Very strong-growing with oval pads that may reach a foot in length. Pads greyish-green, closely set with areoles carrying yellowish-brown glochids. Short golden-yellow spines and long, pale yellow hairs, spreading over surface of pads. Handsome.

O. tuna. Large oval joints with long, straight yellow spines and reddish-yellow flowers. Fruit large and edible – 'prickly pears'.

Nopalea : Tree-like plants with flattened joints and few areoles.

N. coccinellifera. Elongated, bright green joints up to 10 inches long. Spines absent and few areoles with brownish glochids. Flowers bright red. This plant is cultivated as the host plant on which the cochineal scale insect is reared.

Tribe 3. *Cereeae*

All other cacti are included in this tribe, although they differ widely in appearance. They have no glochids and no leaves, even on young plants.

Sub-tribe 1. *Cereanae*

Plants with cylindrical, ribbed stems; erect or sprawling. Flowers funnel-shaped, with a tube.

Cereus : Once a very large genus of over two hundred species, but most have been removed into new genera, although still sometimes found under the old name. Tall, upright columns, branching from base, with ribs. Spines on ribs. Large, funnel-shaped flowers, white inside but greenish or reddish outside. All night-blooming. Very tall-growing, up to 30 feet. Only flower when large – 5 feet or more.

C. azureus, *C. chalybaeus*, and *C. coerulescens*. All deep blue, young growth becoming dark green when older. Spines black.

C. jamacaru and *C. peruvianus*. Both dull green and strong-growing. Cultivation easy in fairly rich soil.

Cephalocereus : Plants with tall columnar stems which, in nature, reach a considerable height. When mature an additional mass of hair is produced at the top of the stem called a pseudo-cephalium.

32. *Cephalocereus senilis*

The flowers are only produced there and are almost hidden in the hair.

C. palmeri. Tall, columnar, and branched. Bluish-green with rounded ribs. Areoles large and woolly, with long greyish hairs. Spines yellow in young plants, black in old ones. Flowers campanulate and pink.

C. polylophus. Columnar with thick stem. Light green when young. Up to thirty acute ribs. Areoles with short yellowish wool and yellow spines. Flowers dark red. Easy and quick-growing.

C. senilis. The 'Old Man' Cactus. Columnar but slow-growing. Areoles produce many soft, hairlike, white bristles which hang down and completely hide stem. Slender, yellow spines hidden by hair. Very popular (Pl. 32).

Cleistocactus: Slender, erect plants branching from base. Numerous ribs and small closely set areoles. Flowers have long, narrow tube, almost closed, with stamens just protruding.

C. baumannii. Areoles yellow with numerous yellowish spines. Flowers over 2 inches long with a curved tube. Bright orange with crimson stamens produced all summer.

C. strausii. Stem slender, up to 3 feet high. Entirely covered with fine white bristles. Long, red flowers only slightly curved. Very fine plant (Pl. 33).

33. *Cleistocactus strausii*, a mountain cactus

34. *Espostoa
huanucensis*

Espostoa : Very hairy or woolly columnar plants from Ecuador and Peru, with a pseudocephalium in which the small, funnel-shaped flowers are almost buried. (A pseudocephalium is a woolly flower-bearing growth near the top of the stem.) Young plants up to a foot high are more attractive than older specimens.

E. lanata. Snow-white, hairy column, but many spines hidden in hairs.

E. dautwitzii. Similar to above but with pale yellow, silky hair, longer and denser at top of column.

E. huanucensis. A recently discovered species similar to *E. lanata*, with white to fox-coloured spines and white silky hair (Pl. 34).

E. ritteri. Branching plant. Dense red radial spines and long black centrals push through the dense white hair.

E. melanostele. The 'Snowball Cactus'. When young like a ball of cotton wool. Older plants columnar and branching from base.

Eulychnia : Tree-like cacti from dry regions of Chile. Most attractive when small, as white, woolly areoles are closely set along the ribs, giving continuous edging of wool. As plants get older, distance between areoles increases so edging is broken up. Long, black spines point in all directions. Give full sun and not much water. *E. iquiquensis* and *E. ritteri* are recommended.

Haageocereus : Columnar or prostrate plants from Peru. Not very tall and branching from base. Closely covered with short, often brightly coloured spines, pale or golden yellow, peach, reddish, violet-brown, or white. The older spines lose these colours. In nature they form long, thick central spines which do not appear on home-grown plants. Night blooming. All have a strong likeness to each other, but some worth-while species with spine colours are : *H. chosicensis*, peach ; *H. c. aureus*, golden ; *H. pseudomelanostele* var. *chrysacanthus*, foxy red ; *H. fulvus*, golden brown ; *H. olowinskianus*, mahogany red.

Harrisia : Tall-growing but slender and sprawling. Can be trained on suitable frame or along greenhouse roof. Flowers large, white, and nocturnal. Ugly plants when not in flower.

*H. bonplandii. Branching stem up to 3 yards long, bluish-green, with spines 1½ inches long. Flowers with long tube ; outer petals brownish, reflexed, long, and narrow ; inner petals broader, snow white ; 10 inches long.

*H. tortuosa. Smaller plant. Stem 3 feet, purplish-green. Stout, spreading, reddish-brown spines. White flowers, 6 inches long.

Heliocereus : Stems slender, branching, three-angled. Large funnel-shaped flowers, strongly scented. Day flowering. Needs warmth and half-shade, with plenty of leaf mould in compost.

H. speciosus. Flowers 6 inches long, shining carmine. Very free-flowering. Used in the original cross with an *Epiphyllum* to give

E. ackermannii and later the many hybrid *Epiphyllums* now to be seen in collections.

H. amecamensis. A white counterpart of the foregoing.

Lemaireocereus: Tall plants branching from base. Large areoles with stout, shortish spines. Flowers smallish, bell-shaped, diurnal, only on very large plants. I find this genus one of the more difficult to keep through the winter as the plants dislike temperatures below 10°C. (50°F.).

L. beneckii. Columnar, unbranched. Stem covered with waxy white bloom. Long spines at first blood-red, later grey. Not easy to grow and best grafted on *Harrisia.* Handsome plant.

*L. chende. Stems thick, deep green, with rounded ribs. Few spines, about ½ inch long. Flowers small, white with pink stripe.

*L. marginatus. Thick, columnar stem, greyish-green with acute ribs. Areoles close together with short greyish wool. Spines short and reddish. Beautiful and quick-growing species.

*L. pruinosus. Few offsets. Stem bluish-green. Ribs acute with prominent knobs. Short, spreading spines, black. Quick-growing.

Lophocereus: Only one species, *L. schottii,* usually seen as the monstrose form, known as the 'Totem Pole Cactus'. Quite spineless, taking strange forms which look as if they had been carved out of jade by a modern sculptor.

Oreocereus: Columnar, very hairy plants from Central Andes. Known as the 'Old Man of the Andes'. Differ from the Mexican 'Old Man' in that the hair at the top forms a long, erect, curly tuft instead of being draped down the sides. Powerful spines push through the hair. The red tubular flowers only appear on old plants.

O. celsianus. Long white hair and yellowish spines. Rather slow-growing (Pl. 35). New varieties have recently been discovered with hair of various colours, in particular one with bright chestnut hair.

O. hendriksenianus. Much quicker growing. Long, silky, yellow hair.

35. *Oreocereus celsianus*. Note the strong spines partly hidden in the long hair

Trichocereus: Large and variable genus. Usually attain a height of 3 feet but sometimes taller. Branching freely from the base, forming big clumps. Flowers large, funnel-shaped, white, nocturnal (Pl. 36).

*T. candicans. Spines yellow and powerful, centrals 4 inches long. Sweet-scented white flowers 10 inches long. Popular.

T. macrogonus. Giant species 9 feet high. Bluish-green with prominent rounded ribs. Large white flowers in groups at top.

*T. schickendantzii. Low-growing and cluster-forming. Spines brownish. Flowers with a very long tube. Easy.

*T. spachianus. Columnar, up to 4 feet high. Shining green with small yellow spines. Free-flowering. Beautiful and popular, also used as grafting stock.

36. A *Tricho-cereus* species discovered by Dr Vatter in northern Argentina and raised from seed of his collecting

Wilcoxia : Stems slender and weak. Large tuberous roots. Young plants difficult until tubers have formed, so usually grafted on a cereus stock. Grafted plants flower freely with fairly large pink or purplish flowers.

W. poselgeri. Spines slender and hairlike, areoles woolly. Flowers funnel-shaped, 2 inches long, pink, lasting for several days.

W. schmollii. Stems hidden under mass of silky white hairs. Flowers purplish-red. Recommended.

Sub-tribe 2. *Hylocereanae*

Epiphytic plants, i.e. growing on forest trees, with long trailing stems. Flowers large and beautiful, with long tubes, usually

37. *Aporocactus flagelliformis*

nocturnal. Most of them need too much room for a small green-house, so only two genera will be described.

Aporocactus: This is the popular 'Rat's Tail Cactus'. The few species are all very similar with slender, trailing stems and red, diurnal flowers. Need rich, open compost and plenty of water in summer.

*A. flagelliformis. Hanging stems up to a yard long (Pl. 37). The long-lasting, cerise, tubular flowers are carried profusely along the stems in May. Often grafted on tall *Pereskia* stock to allow room for tails or else grown in hanging basket.

A. mallisonii, syn. *Heliaporus smithii*, has thicker stems, larger and more open red flowers but not so free-flowering as former. Hybrid between *Heliocereus speciosus* and *A. flagelliformis*.

Selenicereus: Slender, branched, climbing stems with long aerial roots. Spines very short. Flowers large, mainly white, with very long tube, nocturnal.

38. *Selenicereus grandiflorus*, 'Queen of the Night'

S. grandiflorus. Stems up to 15 feet long. Should be grown trained on the wall of a lean-to greenhouse, in rich mixture of leaf mould and loam, and is best given a higher temperature than most cacti. When buds appear in late May needs copious watering until flowers open. Flowers are finest of any cacti. The long tube is curved and 6 inches long. Sepals and petals are in-curved, forming a large cup up to 6 inches long and more across. The numerous, very narrow sepals are nankeen on exterior, pale yellow inside. Petals broad and pure white. Numerous stamens, yellow; and prominent pistil, greenish. Powerful vanilla perfume. Only open after sunset and fade soon after sunrise. Known as 'Queen of the Night' (Pl. 38).

One of parents of modern hybrid *Epiphyllums* which show its influence in their shape and perfume.

S. macdonaldiae. Similar to preceding but flower larger, up to 14 inches long. Largest flower of all cacti.

Sub-tribe 3. *Echinocereanae*

Low-growing plants, often forming large clumps. Most flower when fairly small. Flowers large and brightly coloured.

Chamaecereus : *C. sylvestrii*, only species. The popular 'Peanut Cactus'. Short, cylindrical stems with very short, bristle-like spines. Branches freely. Flowers numerous, funnel-shaped, orange-scarlet. Branches fall off if too dry (Pl. 39). Hybrids with *Lobivia* numerous.

Echinocereus : Numerous species. Stems globular or cylindrical, columnar or clump forming, erect or sprawling. Flowers large and brightly coloured.

E. blanckii. Stems first erect, later sprawling and freely branching from base. Very large, funnel-shaped, violet flowers (Pl. 40).

E. pectinatus. Stem columnar, clusters of numerous, pinkish spines spread comb-like on stem. Large, pink flowers.

E. pentalophus. Stems sprawling, with five warty ribs arranged spirally. Flowers 4 inches long, lilac-pink.

E. reichenbachii. Stem stiff and erect. Flowers when very small, bright pink and numerous. Easy.

39. *Chamaecereus sylvestrii*

40. *Echinocereus blanckii*

87

41. *Echinocereus scheerii*

E. rigidissimus. Upright grower to 12 inches high. Spreading comb-like spines of pale pink and reddish, in alternate layers – hence name 'Rainbow Cactus'. Flowers pink.

*E. salm-dyckianus. Stems numerous, semi-prostrate, dark green. Large flowers, narrowly funnel-shaped, orange-red.

*E. scheerii. Stems semi-prostrate. Flowers 5 inches long, pink. Very free-flowering (Pl. 41).

Echinopsis: Globular plants becoming short and cylindrical with age. Offset freely in many cases all over plant, hiding parent body. Flowers with very long tube and spreading petals, diurnal, short-lived.

*E. eyriesii. Globular, with up to eighteen prominent ribs. Numerous spines from each areole, very short. Flowers 10 inches long, white.

*E. multiplex. Stem globular, pale green. Ribs many and acute. Spines thick, 1½ inches long. Many offsets. Flowers pink.

*E. nigra. Black spines. Flowers white (Pl. 42).

42. *Echinopsis nigra*

43. *Echinopsis (Pseudolobivia) hamatacantha*

E. rhodotricha. Stem cylindrical, up to 2½ feet high. Ribs prominent. Radial spines thick and curved. White flowers freely produced.

E. hamatacantha. Representative of plants sometimes placed in new genus *Pseudolobivia*. Small, globular plants with many ribs and thin, short spines. Very free-flowering, with long tubes and spreading petals (Pl. 43).

Lobivia : Globular or cylindrical, very spiny plants. Flowers large, bell-shaped, with short, wide tubes; red, yellow, or intermediate shades, usually short-lived and open only in sun.

*L. aurea. Much like an *Echinopsis* in appearance and sometimes called *Pseudoechinopsis aurea*. Slender, funnel-shaped flowers, lemon yellow, very freely produced. Better plant than the more expensive, hybrid, yellow echinopses.

44. *Lobivia famatimensis* var. *rosea*

L. famatimensis. Cylindrical with many low ribs. Spines short and yellowish, spreading to cover stem. Flowers huge for size of plant. Many varieties known with flowers of different colours, from pale yellow to deep red (Pl. 44).

L. hertrichiana. Globular, offsetting, glossy green, ribs rounded. Spines curved. Large flowers bright scarlet. Flowers when very small.

L. pentlandii. Globular, freely branching, dark green with prominent ribs. Long curved spines. Flowers in many shades of red. Many named varieties.

L. tegelariana. Globular, offsetting. Spines prominent. Flowers red, very early in season.

Mediolobivia: Small globular plants intermediate between *Lobivia* and *Rebutia*. Bodies often tinged purple or bronze in sun.

45. *Rebutia minuscula*

Buds hairy as in *Lobivia* but open flowers resemble large *Rebutias*.

    **M. aureiflora*. Flowers yellow. Free-flowering.

    M. duursmaiana. Flowers orange with white throat. Needs care.

Rebutia : Small, globular plants, many freely offsetting. Large number of species varying in flower-colour and colour and length of spines. Very free-flowering even when very small. Needs half-shade.

    **R. deminuta*. Somewhat columnar. Hairy buds and large bright red flowers at various parts of plant.

    **R. fiebrigii*. Long white bristle-like spines. Orange flowers.

    **R. marsoneri*. Yellow flowers at base.

    **R. minuscula*. Short white spines and red flowers in ring at base of plant (Pl. 45).

    **R. pseudodeminuta*. Freely offsetting. Fairly large deep red flowers (Pl. 46).

46. *Rebutia pseudodeminuta*

R. senilis. Thickly covered with white bristles. Flowers pale red.

R. xanthocarpa. Short spines and numerous small red flowers at base. Several varieties with salmon, rose, and pale violet flowers (Pl. 47).

Sub-tribe 4. *Echinocactanae*

Globular plants sometimes reaching a very large size. Most with many ribs but some taking strange forms. Flowers from new areoles at top of plant.

Ariocarpus: Low, flat-topped plants, spineless. Large triangular tubercles look like very fleshy leaves. Flowers in centre, rather small.

A. fissuratus. Tubercles broad at base, triangular, grey-fissured, and warty. Called the 'Living Rock' cactus. Flowers pink with darker stripe.

47. *Rebutia xanthocarpa*

Astrophytum: Mainly short columnar, four- or five-sided. Covered with small, white scales. Large yellow flowers with red centres.

A. asterias. Stem flat or dome-shaped with raised, woolly areoles and no spines.

A. capricorne. White scales forming pattern on dark-green background. Long black twisted spines.

A. capricorne var. *senilis.* Spines recurved upwards, ash-grey with age (Pl. 48).

A. myriostigma. Scales so numerous as to colour body pale grey. No spines. Four-sided form known as 'Bishop's Hat' cactus (Pl. 49).

Copiapoa: Globular plants with dense development of wool at top where the yellow campanulate flowers appear. From dry regions of north Chile, so care is needed with watering.

C. cinerea. Forms big clusters. Chalky white with black spines. Very handsome.

48. *Astrophytum capricorne* var. *senilis*

49. *Astrophytum myriostigma*

C. hazeltoniana. Reddish body with orange wool.

C. krainziana. Dull-green body almost hidden by dense growth of white, hairlike spines growing from amidst pale yellow wool.

Denmoza : Low cylindrical plants, many ribbed. Red, tubular, irregular flowers with wool in throat.

D. erythrocephala. Cylindrical, up to 4 feet. Many ribs. Inner spines curved, rusty red, outer spines slender and white. Flower as in *D. rhodacantha* (Pl. 50).

D. rhodacantha. Stem dark green with acute, slightly wavy ribs. Spines blood-red; long, thick, and curved. Red flowers nearly

50. *Denmoza erythrocephala*

51. *Echinocactus grusonii.* Young plant showing warty ribs

3 inches long, tubular; mouth closed, with red stamens and style protruding. Fine plant.

Echinocactus: Very large, up to 3 feet, barrel-shaped cacti. Ribs prominent and spines numerous and strong. Yellow flowers in ring at top.

E. grusonii. Globular, flattened at top. Many thin ribs. Areoles with yellow wool and many strong spines, golden yellow. Young plants have ribs divided into conical warts and straw-coloured instead of golden spines. Very popular plant (Pls. 51 and 52).

52. *Echinocactus grusonii*. Flowering plants showing continuous ribs

53. *Echinomastus macdowellii*

Echinofossulocactus (syn. **Stenocactus**): Fairly small, globular plants with numerous very thin, wavy ribs. Spines large, usually flattened, forming quite an entanglement on top of the plant through which small, mauve, short-tubed flowers have to force their way.

E. coptonogonus. Ribs deeply notched. Spines long, soft, curved upwards, red when young.

Echinomastus: Globular or short cylindrical plants. Low ribs, notched; areoles woolly with very numerous needle-like spines. Flowers purplish.

E. macdowellii. Pale-green body almost hidden by long, snow-white spines, looking like a miniature *Cleistocactus strausii*. Deep-pink flowers at top of plant (Pl. 53).

54. *Ferocactus melocactiformis*

Ferocactus: The 'Barrel Cacti' of the Americans. Thick, strongly spined columns up to 9 feet high, a characteristic feature of Arizona landscape. Young spines brightly coloured, often hooked. Large, bell-shaped, red or yellow flowers form a ring round the top of mature plants. Flowers seldom seen in England.

*F. melocactiformis. Stem blue-green, few ribs when young, but up to twenty-five when adult. Areoles with short wool. Spines pale yellow, red at tips, radials slightly curved, centrals straight and thick, 2½ inches long (Pl. 54).

*F. steinesii. Stem globular, ribs up to twenty, notched into warts. Radial spines slightly curved, centrals more curved. Spines at first ruby-red, later grey. Flowers orange-red. Popular and easy.

55. *Gymnocalycium bodenbenderianum*

Gymnocalycium : Globular plants, some quite large. Ribs notched into tubercles with a protuberance or chin below the areoles, hence the name 'Chin Cactus'. Flowers with short tube covered with scales. Many have strong, curved spines, very beautiful.

G. bodenbenderianum. Stem disc-like, brownish-green, with prominent warts. Spines strong, recurved. Flowers white, flushed pink (Pl. 55).

*G. gibbosum. Low cylindrical, up to 9 inches. Spines slightly curved. Flowers whitish. Blooms when small. The variety *nigrum* has a blackish-green body.

*G. lafaldense. Body small, offsetting freely to form large

101

56. *Gymnocalycium platense*

57. *Leuchtenbergia principis*

clump. Spines slender and bristle-like, flat on body. Flowers violet-pink with darker stripe.

G. mihanovichii. Small, greyish-green flushed red, colour deepening in full sun. Ribs broadly triangular, with deep furrows cut into low warts. Flowers yellowish-white.

*G. platense. Stem globular with prominent warts. Grey wool at areoles. Spines curved and spreading. Flower white with long tube (Pl. 56).

G. venturianum. Chins well marked with yellowish spines flat on body. Slender tubed flowers, bright carmine.

Leuchtenbergia :

L. principis only species. Body small but tubercles very elongated, up to 5 inches, grey-green and triangular. Areoles with greyish wool and papery spines at tips of tubercles. Funnel-shaped flowers, carried on young tubercles, glossy yellow (Pl. 57).

103

58. *Lophophora williamsii*

Lophophora :
  L. williamsii principal species. Glaucous green, globular body, spineless but with wool and papery tufts at areoles. Usually solitary but may offset. Small pink flowers. This is the 'Sacred Mushroom' of the Mexicans. Contains drug which when eaten causes wonderful coloured visions (Pl. 58).

Malacocarpus : Globular plants with very beautiful spine formations. Flowers yellow with scarlet stigmas, freely produced on small plants.
  *M. erinaceus. Many ribs arranged spirally, notched into warts. Areoles with white wool. Yellow flowers 3 inches across.
  M. sellowii. Pale yellow spines forming geometrical pattern over body. Many varieties with differing spine formations.

Matucana : At first consisting of a single species but recently enriched by many beautiful species. Small, globular, with bristly spines and slender, tubular, scarlet flowers.
  M. ritteri. Shining, grass-green body; recurved mahogany spines.
  M. yanganucensis. Body practically covered by network of straw-coloured bristly spines lying flat to form close network.

Neoporteria : Spherical or low cylindrical plants, bristly at top. Flowers pinkish or red.

N. napina. Small body with numerous warts, slightly woolly with very short black spines. Body reddish in sun. Hairy buds open to pinkish-yellow flowers. Little water needed (Pl. 59).

N. nidus. Body entirely covered by long, curved spines, rather soft and hairlike, inner ones directed upwards to form a 'nest' at top of plant. Colour varies in different plants from white through grey to black. Flower reddish with narrow petals. Use very open compost, and keep fairly dry.

Notocactus : Globular or columnar. Flowers usually yellow with red stigma. Very popular plants, easy, free-flowering, and handsome.

59. *Neoporteria napina*

60. *Notocactus concinnus*

61. *Notocactus leninghausii*

N. apricus. Globular, pale green body with slightly notched ribs and curved yellowish spines. Good plant for beginners.

N. concinnus. Stem globular, glossy green with short wool in areoles. Spines pale yellow, bristle-like. Flowers red outside, canary yellow inside (Pl. 60).

N. haselbergii. Makes a ball covered with bristly white spines. Flowers fiery red in bunch at top.

N. leninghausii. Stem tall and cylindrical. Offsets at base. Flat top slants to face sun. Long, hair-like, golden yellow spines with whitish wool at top. Ring of golden flowers on large plants (Pl. 61).

62. *Notocactus ottonis*

63. *Notocactus scopa*

N. ottonis. Very variable. Stem globular, green, with wool at top. Spines spreading, straight or curved, reddish. Flowers glossy yellow (Pl. 62).

N. scopa. Stem cylindrical, pale green covered white bristles, often tipped pink, red, or brown. Rings of canary-yellow flowers (Pl. 63).

64. *Parodia aureispina*

65. *Parodia microsperma*

110

66. *Parodia sanguiniflora*

Parodia : Small plants, globular or cylindrical. Very spiny. Large, brilliantly coloured flowers. Strongly recommended.

*P. aureispina. Small and globular, with straight golden spines and many large golden flowers (Pl. 64).

*P. chrysacanthion. Larger, globular, pale green, with pale-yellow spines forming tuft at top. Smallish yellow flowers freely produced.

P. microsperma. Reddish-brown hooked spines. Flowers pale red outer petals and orange inner ones (Pl. 65).

P. sanguiniflora. Bright-green stem, woolly at top. White, radiating, bristle-like spines with hooked brown centrals. Large, blood-red flowers in group at top. Very beautiful (Pl. 66).

Sub-tribe 5. *Cactanae*

Globular or barrel-shaped. Much wool and bristles produced at top of plants, forming a more or less cylindrical structure called a cephalium, often very tall. Flowers embedded in cephalium. These are tropical plants which need much more heat than average cacti and so are not often seen. They are difficult to obtain, very expensive, and not easy to keep. They are mentioned here because they were the first cacti to be introduced into Europe and have given their name to the whole family.

Melocactus: Globular, straight-ribbed, spiny plants, looking much like an *Echinopsis* before formation of cephalium. Latter gives rise to the common name of 'Turk's Cap Cactus'. Need a very open compost. In winter, temperature should be not less than 16°C. (60°F.). In summer a warm, moist atmosphere is needed.

M. neryi. Body globular, dark green, with broad acute ribs. Greyish spines strongly curved upwards. Cephalium white with long red bristles. Flowers pale pink.

Sub-tribe 6. *Coryphanthanae*

Almost entirely North American. Bodies more or less globular to short cylindrical. Covered with spirally arranged tubercles, with spiny areoles at tips. Flowers from the axils.

Coryphantha: Very close to the better-known mammillarias, but tubercles are grooved along the upper surface from top to base. Flowers much larger than those of mammillaria, usually yellow. In my experience more difficult than mammillarias. Very subject to attack by red spider.

C. cornifera. Body globular, tubercles prominent. Spines strongly recurved. Flowers lemon-yellow.

*C. clava. Body cylindrical, up to 1 foot high and 4 inches thick. Bluish-green in colour, woolly and spiny at top. Flowers 3 inches across, red.

*C. erecta. Shaped as above. Covered with white wool and yellow spines close to the plant body. Large, yellow flowers.

C. vivipara. Most northerly cactus, extending into Canada.

67. *Dolichothele longimamma*

Forms clusters of small, globular bodies, grey in colour with woolly areoles. Flowers 2 inches across, outer petals green, inner ones red.

Dolichothele : Globular plants with very elongated, fleshy, soft tubercles and large yellow flowers.

*D. longimamma. Clustering from base. Large tuberous root. Tubercles up to 3 inches long and $\frac{1}{2}$ inch broad at base. Axils hairy, areoles woolly. Funnel-shaped flowers 2 inches across, canary yellow. Free-flowering (Pl. 67).

*D. melaleuca. Forming clusters when old. Body dark green with thick, obtuse tubercles. Spines recurved. Flowers large, canary yellow (Pl. 68).

*D. sphaerica. Tubercles much smaller than above. Axils bare. Radial spines slender and soft. Single short central spine. Large flowers sulphur-yellow.

68. *Dolichothele melaleuca*

Mammillaria: Plants of this very large genus of over two hundred species are very popular. They remain reasonably small, flower freely when young, and often have showy spine formations. Many are readily propagated by offsets whilst others are easy from seed and have been flowered at a year old. Flowers usually small, but as they form a ring at the top of the plant can be quite showy. In some species large, persistent, red fruits are formed which are as showy as the flowers. All are covered with tubercles, but in some species these are hidden below an abundant growth of hair. Scores of species are offered for sale, but many are very similar. Only the most distinct are mentioned here.

*M. bocasana. Forms large clusters of globular bodies with bristle-like spines, covered with silky white hair. Flowers yellowish with red mid-rib. Long, narrow, scarlet fruits are edible. Very popular.

M. bombycina. Old plants columnar. Spines numerous, centrals hooked. Axils between tubercles filled with white hair. Flowers clear red.

69. *Mammillaria elongata* var. *rufida*

M. elongata. Clusters of cylindrical, usually upright, stems. Spines vary in colour from golden yellow to white, reddish-brown, or mahogany. Flowers white, sparsely produced (Pl. 69).

M. glochidiata. Clusters of small, globular bodies with white bristles and short hooked yellow spines. Flowers pink, showy (Pl. 70).

M. hahniana. Solitary, globular stem flattened at top. Covered with long white bristles. Those at top stand out to form a ruff. Crimson flowers form a ring in the ruff. Recommended.

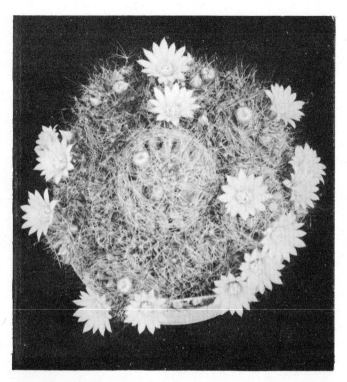

70. *Mammillaria glochidiata*

M. plumosa. Solitary or clustering, globular bodies, entirely covered with feathery white spines. Flowers small, white with red mid-rib. Beautiful species.

M. prolifera (syn. *M. pusilla*). Offsets freely to form large cushion. Small rounded bodies, dark green, soft. Radial spines white and hair-like, centrals strong and yellow. Flowers yellowish, followed by coral-red, globular fruits.

M. rhodantha. One of largest. Cylindrical stem a foot high and 4 inches thick. Prominent spines, slightly curved; yellow, red, or brown according to variety. Flowers brilliant carmine.

M. surculosa. Clusters freely, bodies small and soft. Radial

116

71. *Mammillaria wildii*

spines very thin, glassy, short; centrals hooked, brownish, 1 inch long. Flowers large for genus, sulphur-yellow.

*M. wildii. Clustering heads, low cylindrical, dark green. Tubercles prominent, with white, bristle-like radial spines and stronger, yellow centrals. Flowers whitish with red dorsal band. Easy (Pl. 71).

*M. zeilmanniana. Usually solitary, short cylindric. Radial spines white, soft, and hair-like; centrals hooked, reddish-brown. Flowers nearly an inch across, purplish-red to deep violet. Blooms very early.

Other easy and beautiful species are *M. candida,* **M.*

72. *Mammillaria nunezii*

camptotricha, **M. celsiana*, **M. decipiens*, **M. erythrosperma*, *M. lanata*, **M. microhelia*, *M. nunezii* (Pl. 72), *M. parkinsonii*, and **M. schiediana*.

Thelocactus: Very variable genus of globular, or elongated, solitary bodies; often very spiny. Flowers large, carried on top areoles.

   T. hexaedrophorus. Spherical, solitary stem; up to 6 inches high; covered with large six-sided warts; bluish-green. Spines long, yellowish, darker at tips. Flowers large, white interior, pink exterior (Pl. 73).

Sub-tribe 7. *Epiphyllanae*

Members of this sub-tribe are all forest cacti, some actually growing on trees, others scrambling up them. They are spineless with flattened stems that look like leaves. Flowers are large and showy.

Quite different treatment from the foregoing is needed. Soil

73. *Thelocactus hexaedrophorus*

should be mainly leaf mould and sharp sand. Complete drying-out should be avoided as should also full sun. A north window gives excellent results. Feeding with liquid manure is beneficial.

Nopalxochia phyllanthoides is often called an *Epiphyllum* and is usually seen as the variety 'Deutsche Kaiserin'. It is a bushy, erect plant up to 3 feet high. Flattened stems cylindrical at base, and toothed. Flowers 4 inches long, somewhat campanulate, pink, scented, and freely produced.

There are numerous hybrids, with larger flowers, in pink, red, and orange. All known as *Epiphyllums* but influence of *Nopalxochia* can be seen in shape of flowers.

74. *Schlumbergera gaertneri*

Schlumbergera gaertneri. Low-growing, freely branching. Flattened, oval joints less than an inch long. Joints notched with areoles in notches. End joints terminate in bunch of short yellow bristles. Flowers regular, starlike, 2 inches across, scarlet, in April. Best grafted (Pl. 74).

Zygocactus truncatus. Flat, thin joints that hang over side of pot, and so is often grafted on a tall *Selenicereus* stock. Flowers 3 inches long, irregular with long tube and spreading petals, carmine. Several colour-forms available (Pl. 4).

Epiphyllum: Branches flat and leaf-like, toothed or notched to various amounts, sometimes three-winged. Areoles in notches. Flowers very large, trumpet-shaped. Whilst the narrow, outer petals may be tinged with various colours the broad, inner ones are all pure white in the true species, which are seldom seen.

E. oxypetalum. Branches thin, pointed, undulate. White flowers over a foot long. *E. latifrons* very similar.

Hybrid Epiphyllums (Pl. 75): Many years ago a species of *Epiphyllum* was crossed by *Heliocereus speciosus*. The result was

75. *Epiphyllum* hybrid

the plant known as *Epiphyllum ackermannii* which has the vegetative growth of an *Epiphyllum*, but the red flowers of the *Heliocereus*, produced in dazzling profusion. It is not uncommon for a plant to carry over a hundred blooms. From the point of view of floriferousness it is still the best of the hybrid Epiphyllums (Pl. 76).

Other forest cacti such as *Selenicereus*, *Nopalxochia*, and *Aporocactus* were used to produce other hybrids which were crossed with each other to give a tremendous range of varieties. Borg, writing in 1937, states that there were over 1,000 of these hybrids. Since the war American growers in particular have been

76. *Epiphyllum ackermannii*

producing a steady stream of new-comers in a wide range of colours: white, pink, yellow, scarlet, crimson, carmine, orange, mauve, and violet, with many bicolours. Size and shape also vary, the latter betraying part of the ancestry. The latest American introductions are not only expensive but difficult to obtain owing to import restrictions; but many of the older varieties are still well worth growing.

The following older varieties give a good colour range:

E. 'Cooperi', white; *E.* 'Adonis', pink; *E.* 'William de Laet', carmine; *E.* 'Amber Queen', bright orange; *E.* 'Flamingo', scarlet; *E.* 'Dr Houghton', purple shading to red; *E.* 'Peacockii', carmine with violet throat; *E.* 'Northern Lights', rose with lavender throat; *E.* 'Oriole', yellow and gold with white interior; *E.* 'Sun Goddess', burnt orange with golden sheen; *E.* 'Valencia', orange-yellow darkening to red with violet tones in throat.

'Epiphyllum' is, of course, a misnomer, as quite a number of genera have gone towards the production of these plants. This is

77. *Hatiora salicornioides*

recognized in America, where they are known as 'Orchid Cacti'. The size and range of colour of the flowers puts them well in front of the other cacti from a flowering point of view. They are, in fact, the florist's flowers of the cactus world. But in view of their different vegetative habit and need for different treatment they are best grown apart from the desert cacti. (For cultivation, see pages 30 and 35.)

78. *Rhipsalis cassutha*

Sub-tribe 8. *Rhipsalidanae*

Forest cacti, requiring the same treatment as Sub-tribe 7. The branches may be flattened or leaf-like, cylindrical, angled, or very slender. Spines are usually absent. The flowers are small, followed by juicy berries which are quite ornamental.

Hatiora salicornioides. Low bushes, with small bottle-shaped joints. Branches in whorls. Woolly areoles on terminal joints. Flowers yellow at tips of branches, fruits white berries (Pl. 77).

Rhipsalidopsis rosea. Low, much-branched shrub. Joints three-angled or flat. Purplish in sun. Areoles with bristles. Relatively large flowers produced abundantly at tips of joints, bright pink. Recommended as being free-flowering and beautiful.

Rhipsalis: Large genus, very variable. Much branched with hanging branches. Flowers small, solitary, at areoles along stems.

R. cassutha. Long, thin, cylindrical branches, branching in whorls. Small, yellowish-white flowers at joints. Fruits white berries. Known as 'Mistletoe Cactus'. Native to Africa and Ceylon as well as America (Pl. 78).

R. houlletiana. Flattened, very thin, leaf-like branches. Conspicuous white, funnel-shaped flowers in abundance along edges of branches in winter. Known as 'Snowdrop Cactus'.

R. pentaptera. Pale-green stems with five pronounced angles, winged and toothed. Branches in whorls. Small flowers white with green mid-rib. Fruits pale pink (Pl. 79).

R. platycarpa. Joints leaf-like, notched, dark green with reddish margins. Flowers from side areoles, $\frac{1}{2}$ inch long, yellowish. Fruits greenish-white (Pl. 80).

(B) THE MESEMBRYANTHEMACEAE

At one time a large number of very distinct plants, mainly from South Africa, were gathered together under the genus *Mesembryanthemum*. This word is derived from the Greek *mesos*= middle; *hemera*=day; and *anthemon*=flower. Its meaning is thus 'Midday Flower', in reference to the habit of many of them not opening their flowers until midday. This is by no means universal. As more new plants were discovered and scientifically examined it was found necessary to group them into a large number of

79. *Rhipsalis pentaptera*

80. *Rhipsalis platycarpa*

smaller genera, based on the special characters of flowers and fruits. Some botanists place all these new genera into a special family, the *Mesembryanthemaceae*. In a check list published in 1950, 117 genera and 2,399 species of this family are included, but a considerable number of new plants have been discovered since then. Naturally, only a small percentage of this vast number of plants can be mentioned in a book of this type, but all those commonly available are included.

All can readily be raised from seeds and some of the seedlings will flower during their first year. Some of them are annuals and are now popular as bedding plants. The shrubby types can also readily be raised from stem cuttings.

Whilst many of the genera are very easy to cultivate, some of the very succulent species will test the skill of the best growers. With these, a knowledge of their resting period is essential, and during that time water must be rigidly withheld. They should be grown in full sun, for in many species the flowers only open during sunlight. A very open compost is needed and may contain up to fifty per cent of sharp sand, for stagnant moisture almost certainly causes death. The plants can be divided into roughly three groups:

(1) those with elongated woody stems, erect or prostrate, some of which eventually cover very big areas; (2) low-growing plants with very fleshy leaves on short stems, forming clumps; and (3) highly succulent forms, often with only two leaves to each growth, and even these may be united to form a single body.

Whilst the flowers can, at a casual glance, be mistaken for composites and *Dorotheanthus* is commonly known as 'Livingstone Daisy', closer examination will show that it is a single flower and not a collection of small florets. This becomes clearly apparent when the fruit, a somewhat complicated capsule, appears.

As the species in each genus usually resemble each other closely, in most cases it will be necessary to describe only the genus and not the individual species.

Aptenia: This is a genus of prostrate semi-shrubs with soft branches and stalked, cordate leaves. They have reddish-purple flowers, freely produced in summer and autumn. The best-known is *A. cordifolia* var. *variegata* in which the finely papillose green leaves are heavily marked with creamy-white. It is used as a bedding plant. Keep moderately dry in winter.

Argyroderma : In this genus each growth consists of, at the most, four very fleshy leaves, two from the previous season and two from the new season's growth. As the new leaves expand, the old ones wither away so that in many species at the end of the growing period there are only two leaves forming an almost spherical body. The colour is a silvery grey-green so that the plants mimic the quartz pebbles among which they are found. The stemless flowers form between the leaves and often completely cover the plant. The growing period is in late summer, and water should be withheld until there are signs of growth. If water is given before the plant is ready for it the leaves may split, which will destroy the appearance of the plant. The flowers may be yellow, pink, red, purple, or violet.

The species most commonly seen is *A. octophyllum*, often wrongly named *A. testiculare*, with yellow flowers.

Aridaria : These are much-branched shrubs, the almost prostrate branches heaped up to form cushions. The small, cylindrical leaves are pale green, slightly frosted, and with a few dark-green tubercles. The large flowers, at the ends of the branches, are solitary and whitish in colour. The best-known species is *A. splendens*. The growing period is in the summer.

Bergeranthus : These stemless, very succulent plants have crowded, upright leaves in rosettes. A number of these rosettes form a large clump. The leaves are triangular in shape, glabrous, and grey-green in colour. The golden-yellow flowers have stalks up to 4 inches in length, and appear in early summer. The growing period is in summer and they should be kept fairly dry in winter. The best-known species is *B. multiceps*.

This is one of the less interesting of the non-shrubby genera.

Cheiridopsis : These are highly succulent plants formed of a number of growths, each of which usually has two leaves, the leaves of the previous season drying up to envelop the base of the new pair in a kind of sheath. In several of the better-known species the new leaves stand up like bunches of fingers. The colour is usually whitish or grey-green. The solitary flowers are yellow and usually stalked. Propagation is best from seeds, as cuttings do not root readily. The growing period is usually from late summer to winter, but after Christmas they should be kept very dry and moderately warm. *C. candidissima* is one of the handsomest with boat-shaped leaves united for nearly half their length of nearly 4 inches. In a sunny position they are practically white. *C. cigarettifera* and *C. marlothii* are similar. *C. peculiaris* is quite different, its two leaves, united at the base, being prostrate. They are about 2 inches long and wide, tapering abruptly to a point. A new pair of leaves (which are completely united) is developed for the resting period. Seed germinates readily, but it is not too easy to bring the plants to maturity.

Conophytum : This is a large genus of over two hundred species, but many are very similar to each other. They are very dwarf, only a few forming stems when old. The growths consist of small, fleshy bodies formed of two leaves joined together to make a spherical to cylindrical object across which a tiny fissure can be seen. The genus can be divided into two groups, one with more or less spherical bodies, the other with the bodies more cylindrical and with two distinct lobes. These bodies multiply rapidly and a large mound is soon formed. The flowers may be white, yellow, pink, carmine, or violet, and are often very large for the size of the body producing them. For example, in *C. minutum* the body is only $\frac{1}{4}$ inch in diameter, but the violet flowers may be $\frac{3}{4}$ inch across. The flowers are produced in abundance, one flower from the centre of each body.

The new bodies are produced inside the old ones, withdrawing the material from the old body until nothing is left but the dry skin. This happens between May and August, by which time the plant looks quite dead. Water must not be given during this period, and watering is only restarted when the swelling of the new body bursts the dry skin. Growth does not last for many weeks, after which water is again restricted for the winter.

81. *Conophytum nelianum*

Watering can be done from March to May, when the new bodies are forming.

Propagation is easy from cuttings, taken in spring, or from seeds. Seedlings will flower in their second year. In this genus succulence reaches its extreme limit and so it is one of the most popular in the family. Provided the rules for watering are followed, they are of easy cultivation. Suitable species are *bilobum, elishae, meyerae, nelianum* (Pl. 81), *pallidum* (Pl. 82), *truncatellum, tischeri,* and *velutinum.*

82. *Conophytum pallidum*

Corpuscularia: These are very succulent plants with prostrate branches and short, thick leaves in pairs. The leaves are grey-green in colour and united at the base. The large red or yellow flowers are formed at the ends of the shoots in summer. They are easily grown. *C. *taylori* is the best known.

Delosperma: This is a genus of shrubby plants showing more variation between the species than most. Their growing period is summer when they may be bedded out. Cuttings root easily and

soon make flowering specimens. The best-known species is
D. echinatum, which has leaves the shape of a rugger ball
opposite each other. They are pale green and covered with short
bristles. The freely produced flowers are pale yellow. *D. aber-
deenense* is becoming popular. It hangs over the sides of the pot
and gives a succession of showy carmine flowers.

Dinteranthus: These highly succulent plants are usually seen as
single bodies but may form clumps when old. The short, thick
leaves are united at the base and almost flat at the top. The
whitish surface is glabrous and either unmarked or covered with
numerous greenish dots. The large yellow flowers appear in
summer. Watering should be done sparingly at all times and none
given in winter. Recommended species are *D. inexpectatus*,
D. microspermus, and *D. pole-evansii*.

Dorotheanthus: This genus of annuals is now very well known
to the gardening public as a bedding plant. *D. criniflorus* has
white, pink-tipped flowers (Pl. 21), whilst *D. gramineus* has
carmine flowers with a darker centre; but the seeds now offered
by several firms will give a much wider range of colours.

Drosanthemum: These shrubby plants may grow fairly tall. The
slender, plentifully branched stems are covered with shining
papillae, and the red or white flowers are very freely produced in
summer. Cultivation is easy and cuttings root readily. *D. hispi-
dum*, with purple-red flowers, and *D. speciosum*, with bright
orange-red flowers, are two of the best species.

Faucaria: These low-growing, very succulent plants, are popular with collectors. There are a considerable number of species
but, with one exception, very similar to each other. The crowded
leaves are keeled and triangular in cross-section, with softish teeth
all along the margins which give rise to the specific names:
F. felina (cat), *F. lupina* (wolf), and *F. tigrina* (tiger). The large
yellow flowers appear in autumn. The growing period is in
autumn and winter when watering needs to be carried out, and
they should therefore be kept dry in summer. Whilst cultivation

83. *Faucaria tuberculosa*

is relatively easy, the plants are very prone to attack by mealy bugs, which shelter round the crowded bases of the leaves.

F. tuberculosa, in addition to the teeth along the edges, has the upper surface of the leaves covered with tooth-like warts (Pl. 83).

Fenestraria : This genus is the most prominent of the so-called 'window plants'. The plant consists of a clump of club-shaped, fleshy leaves which, in their native habitat, are buried in the sand so that only the slightly rounded top protrudes. This end of the leaves is almost transparent and without chlorophyll, enabling light to penetrate to the inside of the leaves where carbon assimilation takes place. The growing period is in summer, but even

133

84. *Fenestraria rhopalophylla* showing windows at tips of leaves

then the soil must not be kept wet. In winter keep quite dry. The compost should be very sandy and repotting is resented by the plant. If a larger pot is necessary do not disturb the ball of roots. There are only two species, *F. aurantiaca* with orange flowers, and *F. rhopalophylla* with white ones (Pl. 84).

Frithia : This genus has a single species, *F. pulchra*. It is very similar to *Fenestraria* in appearance but its growing period is in winter and it needs to be kept dry in summer. The carmine, white-centred flowers appear in March. While it is raised from seeds and brought to flower easily, survival after a first flowering is by no means certain.

Gibbaeum: This is another highly succulent genus, but shows considerable variation in the form of the bodies. They vary in form from ovate or spherical to cylindrical. They may be slightly notched to definitely divided, the lobes being even or uneven. The leaves may be united or quite separate from each other. It is one of the more difficult genera and the various species need individual treatment as their growing periods vary. At all times water must be given in moderation, the soil never remaining saturated, and during the resting period they must be kept quite dry. They are best raised from seeds which germinate in less than a week. *G. album* has unequal leaves united to form an obliquely ovate body. The glabrous surface is covered with minute hairs and the large flower is white. The growing period is summer. *G. dispar* has bodies of two unequal leaves with a very deep fissure between them. They are grey-green, flushed with brown, and covered with fine hairs. The flower is deep lilac, in August. *G. pubescens* has short, woody, branching stems each with two to three pairs of branching leaves, united at the base but spreading. The two leaves of a pair are of unequal lengths, one being three times as long as the other. They are whitish-grey, owing to a covering of fine, felted hairs pressed close to the surface of the leaf. The stalked flowers are violet-red, in February. The growing period is in late winter. *G. velutinum* has leaves united at the base but widely spreading, more or less prostrate on the ground and tapering to a point. The colour is pale bluish-green and the white flowers appear in April. The growing period is the first half of the year.

Glottiphyllum: These low-growing, very succulent plants are very easy to grow. Owing to their readiness to hybridize and the fact that they are usually grown from seeds, few of the plants in cultivation are true species.

The leaves are often arranged in two rows, flat on the ground. They are tongue-shaped, usually three or more times as long as they are wide. Fresh green in colour, they are soft and often flabby to the touch. The large flowers are golden yellow. The growing period is the latter half of the year, but at no time should much water be given or they develop vigorously and soon grow out of character. They can be bought under a variety of names – *G. latum*, *G. longum*, *G. linguiforme*, and so on – but they all look alike. This, of course, does not apply to imported plants, but the genus is not sufficiently popular with connoisseurs for these to be seen often.

Lampranthus: This is a genus of small shrubs, erect or prostrate, with small, more-or-less cylindrical, pointed leaves. They carry quantities of fair-sized flowers in many different colours all summer and can be used as bedding plants. Cuttings root readily and soon make good plants. Useful species, with flower colours, are *L. aurantiacum*, shining orange; *L. aureum*, golden yellow; *L. blandum*, pink; *L. brownii*, dull orange-red; *L. coccineum*, scarlet; *L. conspicuum*, purple-red; *L. glomeratum*, violet; *L. roseum*, pale pink; *L. tenuifolium*, orange-scarlet.

Lithops: These, the so-called 'Living Stones', are the most popular and interesting of the whole family. For once, the popular name is really apt as they are so much like the small pebbles among which they grow that they are difficult to find. There are about seventy species, all similar in shape and habit of growth, but differing in colour and markings.

Each plant-body is almost cylindrical, made up of two almost completely united leaves with a small fissure across the top from which the almost stemless flower emerges. The greater part of the body is buried, leaving the nearly flat top exposed. The markings act as windows to allow light to penetrate into the interior of the body.

The growing period is from April onwards, when new bodies are in process of formation. The old bodies gradually shrink until only a dry skin is left, through which the new bodies burst their way. Sometimes two new bodies form inside one old one and in this way clumps are built up. During summer the compost should be kept moist, but after flowering, from July to October, watering should be carried out less and less frequently, and from late October to March the plants should be kept quite dry. A very sandy soil should be used and only the lower third of the cylindrical body should be buried in it.

85. *Lithops salicola*

As Lithops grow in very dry desert regions, unprotected from the blazing sun, they need the sunniest position available. There is no fear of their being scorched, since in Africa they have to withstand temperatures of 120° F. The use of small pots is not advocated as the roots might be burnt. If used they should be plunged in sand or gravel. It is common practice to grow a number in large pans, when the plants are surrounded by pebbles of similar colouring. This emphasizes the similarity of the plants to stones.

Propagation is best by seeds, although cuttings can be used when the clump is large enough, if seeds are not available.

The following are some of the most distinct species: *L. alpina*, pale brown with brown markings; *L. bella*, brownish-yellow; *L. comptonii*, olive-green; *L. fulleri*, dove-grey with brownish-violet markings; *L. karasmontana*, pale bluish-yellow with ochre markings; *L. kuibisensis*, reddish; *L. laterita*, brick-red; *L. lesliei*, coffee-coloured with dark greenish markings; *L. olivacea*, olive-green flecked white; *L. optica rubra*, purple-red with very prominent windows; *L. pseudotruncatella*, brownish-grey, flushed and marbled brown; *L. salicola*, elephant grey, with greenish

86. *Ophthalmophyllum friedrichiae*

markings (Pl. 85); *L. turbiniformis*, brownish with dark-brown lines and warty protuberances.

Nananthus: These are small plants with four to six leaves to a growth. The leaves are spreading, more or less lanceolate, keeled below, covered with wart-like dots. The nearly sessile flowers are yellow. The growing period is in summer.

The best-known species are *N. pole-evansii* and *N. vittatus*.

Ophthalmophyllum: This is another genus of highly succulent plants, usually with only a single shoot. The body consists of two united leaves, forming a cylinder with a fissure across the top. The lobes have large, transparent windows, and there are also transparent dots down the sides. As with *Lithops*, the old bodies dry up to form a skin which protects the young body from too much sun. The flowers are white, pink, or lilac. The growing period is in winter. When resting they must be kept absolutely dry. Propagation is by seed and even the young seedlings must have their resting period. Recommended species are *O. dinteri*, *O. friedrichiae* (Pl. 86), *O. pillansii*, and *O. schlechteri*.

138

Oscularia: These shrubby plants have prostrate branches and in nature will form mats a yard across. They are of the easiest culture and free-flowering. The small leaves are three-angled, toothed along the edges, and grey-green in colour. The flowers are pink or red.

Propagation is best from cuttings, which soon make flowering plants. The growing period is in spring and summer. They make useful house plants.

The best-known species is *O. deltoides*.

Pleiospilos: These are mimicry plants, very highly succulent, and resembling pieces of blue-green granite. The leaves are usually in two pairs, the new ones growing and the old ones gradually withering away. Most of the species gradually form clumps by division, but the most attractive remain as a single head. For most species the growing period is from August to December, but *P. nelii* flowers in early spring. During the rest of the year the

87. *Pleiospilos nelii*

88. *Pleiospilos simulans*

plants must be kept dry. The large usually golden flowers are practically sessile. Propagation is by seeds, but as the different species hybridize readily, home-saved seed should not be used. *P. nelii* is the most popular. It is almost spherical with a deep fissure separating the two leaves which are blue-green and nearly smooth, but with a few raised dots (Pl. 87). The flower is apricot-coloured. *P. bolusii* is very similar. *P. simulans* usually has two leaves, brownish-green, fleshy, spreading, triangular, and flat on the upper side, with a keeled back. The flowers range from yellow to orange (Pl. 88). In other species the leaves are more boat-shaped and more widely separated.

Rhombophyllum: These are tufted, succulent plants, with crowded leaves. The sap-green leaves with whitish dots are flat on the upper surface and keeled below, the lower surface being drawn forward to form a chin-like protuberance at the tip. Numerous golden yellow flowers are given on the same stalk during summer. The growing period is from June to November. Propagation is by seed.

The best-known species is *R. rhomboideum*.

Ruschia: This is a very large genus of shrubby plants, either erect or prostrate. They vary widely in appearance from the dwarf cushions of *R. amoena* to taller shrubs up to $1\frac{1}{2}$ feet high or more. The flowers are often on the small side, from white through shades of pink and red to purple. The taller kinds offer no difficulty but the tufted species dislike too much water. Propagation is easy by cuttings.

R. uncinata is reasonably hardy and can be grown outside on the rock garden in most parts of the country except in severe winters.

Sceletium: These are prostrate small shrubs, the leaves being pale green in colour and not particularly succulent. The old leaves are persistent and become almost skeletonized whilst still on the plant. The flowers are fairly large, white or pale yellow, from March onwards. Propagation is by seeds or cuttings.

Species usually seen are *S. anatomicum* and *S. concavum*.

89. *Titanopsis calcarea*

Stomatium: These are dwarf plants, forming clumps with very short stems. The grey-green leaves are semi-cylindrical in section near the stalk, but are keeled towards the tip. The edges have short, broad teeth and the upper surface is covered with small tubercles. The short-stalked or sessile flowers are yellow and appear in spring and summer. These easily grown plants can be propagated by seeds or cuttings.

The best-known species are **S. erminium* and *S. suaveolens*.

Titanopsis: These stemless, clump-forming, very succulent plants are some of the most interesting in the family. The rosettes of very crowded leaves are blue-green, turning reddish or

90. *Titanopsis setifera*

yellowish-white in the full sun. The surface of the leaves is covered with prominent warts. They are mimicry plants, an old clump having the appearance of a weathered, cracked piece of limestone. The almost stemless flowers are yellow or orange.

The growing period is in the summer, but water should be given carefully at all times since if it lodges between the leaves it may cause decay. Propagation is by seeds.

The best-known species is *T. calcarea* (Pl. 89), but *T. primosii*, *T. schwantesii*, and *T. setifera* (Pl. 90) are possibly more handsome as young plants. Certain species formerly considered to be *Titanopsis* have now been removed to *Nananthus*, and there is a strong resemblance between the two genera.

91. *Trichodiadema densum*

Trichodiadema: This genus of twenty-eight species consists of low bushes with small leaves glistening with papillae. A distinguishing feature is the cluster of small bristles at the tips of the leaves. This feature has, on more than one occasion, been mistaken for the areole of a cactus, and plants at shows have been entered in the wrong class. The medium-sized red or white flowers are freely produced over a long period. The plants have only a short resting period in January and February, and require plenty of water when growing. Propagation is best from cuttings, which is quicker than from seed.

The most popular species is *T. densum* with red-violet flowers (Pl. 91), but *T. mirabile*, with mahogany-tipped leaves and white flowers, is well worth growing.

(C) OTHER SUCCULENTS

Family Agavaceae

Agave : This is a genus containing over three hundred species, but few are suitable for the average collection as they reach very large proportions. They are unlikely to flower in this country as they take many years to reach flowering size, but along the Riviera, where they have become naturalized, the dead flower-spikes may be seen looking like telegraph poles. The plant dies after flowering.

The leaves are arranged in rosettes and are very stiff, usually toothed and ending in a sharp spine. This makes them difficult to fit into the small greenhouse. The bigger species are best grown in tubs, placed outside during the summer and put in a frost-proof shed for the winter. In the milder parts of the country they may be planted outside in a sheltered situation.

Most species produce many offsets which can usually be pulled off with roots attached for propagating. Some of them form young plants in the axils of the flowering spikes, and all can be readily grown from seeds.

*A. americana. Rosette of over 6 feet in diameter. Typical plant blue-green. Offsets freely. Flower spike up to 24 feet high with twenty-five to thirty side-shoots at right angles carrying masses of 3-inch-long yellowish flowers. Numerous varieties with leaves striped with gold, white, greenish-yellow, pale green, or pink. They make good tub plants for a terrace.

*A. filifera. Small species. Narrow, shiny green leaves with white lines. Horny band at edge splits into many long threads.

A. parrasana. Rosette almost spherical, without offsets. Wide leaves taper abruptly to a short point. Edges toothed and sinuous. Pale bluish-green with dark spines. Beautiful species.

A. parryi. Shiny, grey-green rosette without offsets; 2 feet in diameter. Flower stem grows to 15 feet high with curved ascending branches carrying many 1½-inch-long cream-yellow flowers. Almost hardy.

*A. stricta. Almost spherical rosette of stiff, slightly incurved linear leaves; 1 foot long with long terminal spine.

A. victoriae-reginae. Leaves 6 inches long, 2 inches wide, incurved. Dark green with oblique white lines. Terminal spine very short. Does not offset (Pl. 92).

92. *Agave victoriae-reginae*

Family Asclepiadaceae : Tribe *Stapelieae*

The Stapelieae are leafless plants with the single exception of
Frerea indica, seldom seen in collections. They have very fleshy
stems and, in many cases, large, strangely shaped flowers. Many
of the flowers have a strong smell of carrion. They are fertilized
by flies. A very open compost is needed. Half leaf mould and
half sharp sand is suitable. The top inch should be pure sand as
the plants have a tendency to rot at the collar. Full sun should be
avoided. They are readily propagated from seeds or cuttings,
but the latter must be dried for some days before planting.

Caralluma : Low shrubs with fleshy stems, usually four-angled,
and with soft teeth along the angles. The flowers are often small,
carried in bunches at the upper parts of stems. They should be

93. *Caralluma subterranea*

viewed through a magnifying glass for the queer shapes and colours to be appreciated. The seed pods are like horns, several inches long.

*C. europaea. Branches spreading, almost square in section. Greyish-green with a few reddish markings. Flowers in sessile umbels; greenish-yellow heavily marked with reddish-brown cross-lines, blackish-brown at centre. Near the centre are ten yellow, knob-like excrescences. Flowers almost continuously.

C. lugardii. Stems almost prostrate or creeping underground like offsets, four-angled, and dark green with brown flecks. Edges blunt with erect teeth. Flowers 2 inches in diameter, in umbels, bell-shaped at base, tips narrow and tapering, brown at base, greenish-yellow at lobes, fine hairs inside and on margins.

C. subterranea. Stems 3 inches high. Flowers dark brown to citron-yellow with fine silvery hairs (Pl. 93).

Duvalia : Clusters of prostrate, four-angled stems, short and thick, edged by small teeth. Flowers five pointed stars with inner ring in contrasting colour. The sixteen species closely resemble one another.

D. elegans. Flowers $\frac{3}{4}$ inch in diameter, blackish-violet with long, purple hairs.

D. pillansii. Flowers greenish outside, purple-brown inside with yellowish ring. Interior with reddish hairs.

Hoodia : Very fleshy stemmed shrubs up to $2\frac{1}{2}$ feet. Cylindrical ribbed stems carry many hard, thorn-like teeth. Flowers at top of stems, large, saucer-shaped with six points, whitish or flesh-coloured. Best grown in a double pot, watering only outer one. Sometimes grafted on Stapelias.

H. bainii. Stems covered with tubercles, ending in long, woody spines (Pl. 7). Flowers bell-shaped, slightly five lobed, dull yellow, fading to reddish.

Huernia syn. **Heurnia :** Low-growing, with four- to six-angled stems, with large soft teeth. Coloured various shades of grey-green tinged red. Flowers at bases of young stems, bell-shaped with ring-like inner corolla in centre.

H. keniensis. Stems green passing to red, 4 inches long and $\frac{1}{2}$ inch thick. Flower bell-shaped, reddish purple, inner corolla purple and hairy.

H. pillansii. Stems only $1\frac{1}{2}$ inches high covered with tubercles ending in long hairs. Bell-shaped flower with elongated lobes, pale yellow with red flecks.

H. primulina. Stems four-sided, 3 inches high, with small teeth along angles, pale grey-green. Bell-like flower, primrose-yellow with almost black inner corolla surrounded by reddish markings.

Piaranthus : Prostrate, very succulent plants similar to *Duvalia*. Jointed stems root as they grow, making propagation easy. Flowers small with bell-shaped tube and five acute triangular lobes.

P. foetidus. Stems elliptical with warty teeth, grey-green tinged red. Flowers yellow with red lines.

148

94. *Piaranthus globosus*

*P. *globosus*. When grown in the sun looks, in both shape and colour, like a pile of small new potatoes. Starry flowers are greenish-yellow with red or lilac flecks (Pl. 94).

Stapelia : Large genus of about a hundred species and many varieties. Hybridize freely, so many of plants in commerce not true to name. All species have very fleshy stems, usually erect but sometimes pendant. Stems four-angled, angles coarsely toothed, branching at base to form large clumps. Flowers at base of young stems, bell-shaped, divided at top into five spreading or recurved lobes, rather fleshy, with thick fleshy ring in middle.

S. *asterias*. Star-shaped flowers, dull purple with transverse yellow markings and edged with white hairs.

S. *bella*. Erect stems to 8 inches. Flowers 2 inches across, lobes recurved, pale yellow with many reddish-brown cross-markings, pale brown hairs round edges.

149

95. *Stapelia hirsuta*

S. gigantea. Flowers up to 1 foot in diameter, lobes with greatly elongated tips like gigantic starfish, pale yellow with many thin, wavy red stripes and red hairs.

S. grandiflora. Flowers 6 inches, with deeply cleft lobes, blackish purple with long silvery hairs at edges.

*S. hirsuta. Stems slender, sooty-green, with small hairs. Flowers up to 5 inches across, deeply divided, with reddish hairs at edges, pale yellow with deep red wavy stripes (Pl. 95).

S. maculosa. Flowers flat, lobes somewhat triangular, yellow with thick red marks and blotches. Centre ring somewhat darker.

*S. variegata. Low-growing with pendant stems. Flowers 2 inches, lobes triangular and slightly recurved, ring prominent (Pl. 96). Typical flower ochre-yellow marbled purple, but var. *bufonia* has brown flowers with black markings, and var. *marmorata* has dark brown flowers with yellow markings.

96. *Stapelia variegata*

Family Compositae

These plants may be stem or leaf succulents. They may have the familiar daisy flowers or else the rayless flowers similar to those on the well-known weed, groundsel.

Kleinia : Succulent sub-shrubs, erect or prostrate, deciduous or evergreen. Flowers terminal, solitary or in corymbs, rayless. Grow in rich, open compost. Propagate from cuttings.

97. *Kleinia
neriifolia*

*K. articulata. The 'Candle Plant'. Stems erect, cylindrical, jointed, covered by grey, waxy bloom. Small leaves in autumn but soon wither. Yellowish flowers in corymbs. Growing period in winter.

K. gomphophylla. Stems prostrate, rooting from nodes. Small, very fleshy leaves shaped like rugby balls, light green with translucent stripes to allow penetration of light, reddish in full sun. Flowers small, solitary, whitish.

*K. neriifolia. Bushes up to 10 feet high, freely branched. Branches cylindrical, white waxy coating with darker lines. Leafless in summer but in autumn rosette of long, elliptical leaves form, 6 inches long, grey-green. Yellow flowers in corymbs (Pl. 97). Keep dry in summer; water once a week in winter.

Othonna : Mostly small shrubs with succulent stems. Flowers yellow daisies.

*O. crassifolia. Long, thin, branching, hanging stems. Narrow, cylindrical leaves, 1 inch long, persistent, pale grey-green, becom-

98. *Othonna herrei*

ing purplish in sun. Flowers small yellow daisies in autumn. Good plant for a hanging basket.

O. herrei. Stem short, thick, warty with remains of old leaves. Leaves at ends of branches, thick, oval with irregular teeth, blue-green, 2 inches long in winter, deciduous in summer. Keep dry in summer; water in winter when the leaves flag. Flowers several to a stem, yellow (Pl. 98).

Senecio : Huge genus, including weeds, herbaceous plants, shrubs, and even trees. Many succulent species, usually leaf succulents, varying in form, many with large tuberous roots. Cultivation as for *Kleinia.*

S. fulgens. Stem erect, fleshy, swollen at base. Large tuberous

99. *Adromischus festivus*

root, so a deep pot is needed. Leaves large, spatulate, bluish-green with white overlay, sometimes tinged purple, persistent. Flowers in winter: large, rayless, bright red.

S. scaposus. Stemless rosette of upright, incurved, cylindrical leaves, 2 inches long, grey-green with white felted coating when young. Flowers yellow. Growing period summer, dry in winter.

S. stapeliiformis. Stems five-angled, greyish with dark green stripes, rudimentary, thorny leaflets at angles. Flowers terminal, rayless, bright red. Resting period summer. Water about once a fortnight in the winter growing period.

Family Crassulaceae

This is a very large family containing many well-known genera of succulents. They vary enormously in character.

Adromischus: Low-growing leaf succulents from the Cape and Namaqualand. Flowers insignificant, white or pink, in terminal spikes. Easily propagated by leaf cuttings. Water when the soil appears very dry in winter, as if the plants are kept too dry leaves may drop.

A. clavifolius. Low-growing with club-shaped leaves, thick and truncate, light green.

A. cooperi. Leaves roundish-spatulate, blue-green with darker markings. One of the best.

A. festivus.* Leaves egg-shaped, blue-green with mahogany markings, colour justifying popular name of 'Plover's Eggs' (Pl. 99).

A. maculatus. Flat, roundish, grey-green leaves marked with reddish-brown on both sides which pile up to form a handsome, shining mound.

Aeonium: Rosette plants with rosettes carried on tall stems, either solitary or branching. Most species have terminal, branching sprays of bright golden flowers, but there are other colours. The solitary species die after blooming but may be propagated by leaf cuttings taken before flowers are too far advanced. If plants become too leggy the tops may be removed and rooted as cuttings. The stumps put out fresh shoots. Grow in full sun to bring out foliage colours. Give plenty of water in summer and also some in winter.

A. arboreum. Branching shrub up to 3 feet. Rosettes of spatulate leaves at ends of branches. Foot-high racemes of golden flowers.

A. arboreum atropurpureum.* Leaves blackish-red in full sun.

A. arboreum albo-variegatum.* Rosettes of white mottled leaves, often mistaken for flowers. Very good (Pl. 100).

A. caespitosum. Low-growing and well branched. Lanceolate leaves, fresh green with reddish stripes. Flowers deep yellow. Resting period in summer when leaf rosettes close up.

A. domesticum. Low mound. Fleshy leaves almost round and covered with fine hairs. Very free-flowering with short, few-flowered racemes of golden flowers. Variegated form has white mottled leaves.

100. *Aeonium arboreum albo-variegatum*

A. haworthii. Freely branching with numerous aerial roots. Pointed leaves blue-green with reddish margins, slightly toothed. Flowers whitish.

A. tabulaeforme. Very distinct. Flat, plate-like rosette of overlapping, grass-green leaves reaching diameter of 20 inches. In old plants a thick branching inflorescence is pushed up from centre of rosette to height of 2 feet. Flowers sulphur-yellow.

A. urbicum. Single, tall stem with aerial roots. Leaves spatulate with reddish margins. Flowers pale pink (Pl. 101).

101. *Aeonium urbicum*

102. *Cotyledon wallichii*

Bryophyllum: Small shrubs with succulent leaves. Edges of leaves carry little plantlets which drop off and root easily. Terminal, many flowered umbels of tubular flowers. Flowering shoot dies after blooming, but new shoots form from base. Use rich compost.

*B. crenatum. Oval, toothed, glaucous leaves, edged red. Adventitious buds in notches (Pl. 14). Red flowers in winter.

*B. daigremontianum. Pointed leaves 5 inches long and 2 inches wide, toothed, with adventitious buds in notches. Upper side of leaf shining green, under side irregularly flecked brown. Yellow to pink flowers in winter.

*B. tubiflorum. Linear leaves, almost cylindrical in section but grooved on upper surface, 5 inches long, in whorls of three. Adventitious buds, pale pink, flecked green, at ends of leaves (Pl. 15). Orange flowers in winter.

Cotyledon: Shrubs with succulent leaves and sometimes very swollen stems. Divided into two distinct sections, evergreen and

103. *Cotyledon ladismithensis*

deciduous. The former have their growing season in summer, the latter in winter. Flowers are produced from centres of rosettes which die after flowering. The flowers are bell-shaped in shades of orange.

*C. orbiculata. Vigorous, branching shrub. Leaves roundish, thick, grey-green with white, waxy coating; often edged red. Leaf form very variable. Flowers in tall umbels, tubular, yellowish-red.

C. paniculata. Thick, fleshy, conical stem when young but branching when adult to height of 5 feet. Leaves narrow lanceolate, fleshy, bright green, deciduous in summer, formed in October. Red flowers during summer. Other similar species are *C. reticulata*, *C. ventricosa*, and *C. wallichii* (Pl. 102).

*C. undulata. Usually single stemmed. Leaves fleshy, obovate, with undulate edges, thickly covered with white farina. Flowers bell-shaped, orange with few red stripes. Usually dies after flowering. Beautiful.

Other species worth growing are *C. barbeyi*, *C. coruscans*, *C. ladismithensis* (Pl. 103), *C. macrantha*, and *C. teretifolia*.

159

104. *Crassula anomala*

Crassula : Very large genus of shrubby plants, varying from dwarfs to tall shrubs. Includes many easy and very popular species, but also difficult rarities, which are not described here. Individual flowers small, but collected into inflorescences are quite showy. Colour varies. Most can be propagated from leaf cuttings.

C. anomala. Small sub-shrub; leaves bluntly spatulate, dark green, turning bronze-red in sun. Small white flowers collected in spherical heads (Pl. 104).

*C. arborescens. Strong-growing shrub, up to 6 feet. Leaves large, roundish, very fleshy, grey-green with red margin and red spots on upper surface. Seldom flowers here.

*C. argentea syn. *C. portulacea*. Shrub with fleshy, gnarled trunk. Leaves 1½ inches long with short tip, shining green. Numerous flowers, large for genus, pale pink, in April.

*C. cooperi syn. *C. bolusii*. Low cushion. Leaves small, lanceo-

105. *Crassula lycopodioides*

late, pale green with darker markings, in small rosettes. Flowers in small heads on short stalks, flesh pink, in winter.

C. justus-corderoy. Low clump of fleshy, lanceolate leaves, grey-green, flecked brown, covered with short hairs. Large heads of small, deep-pink flowers, in summer.

C. lactea. Shrub up to 2 feet. Fleshy, pointed leaves united in pairs at base, bright green with white dots round edge. Sprays of white, starry flowers, large for a crassula, in winter. Useful house plant.

C. lycopodioides. Sub-shrub, up to 1 foot. Irregularly branched, slender stems covered with four rows of scale-like, clasping leaves. Minute flowers in axils of leaves have strong, unpleasant smell. There are cristate, monstrose, and variegated forms (Pl. 105).

C. perforata. Shrub forming cluster of unbranched stems up to 18 inches. Leaves broadly united at base in pairs, pale grey-green. Small, pale yellow flowers in spikes at tips of branches.

161

106. *Dudleya brittonii*

C. rupestris. Prostrate edition of former. Good for hanging baskets.

C. nealeana syn. *C. rupestris minor*. Miniature edition of *C. rupestris*. Free-flowering. Very good.

C. tetragona. Tall-growing shrub with slender branches. Linear, pointed leaves almost cylindrical, 1 inch long. Useful for bowl gardens. Twigs fall if too dry.

Besides the foregoing there are some interesting dwarf species, more difficult and suited for the more advanced collector. They include *C. barbata*, *C. columnaris*, *C. deceptrix*, *C. hemisphaerica*, and *C. teres*.

Dudleya : Rosette plants from Mexico and California. Become leggy when old, but may be cut back and rerooted. Most species are heavily coated with white farina. Flowers on long, straggly stalks, tubular. Growing period winter and early spring. Need full sun.

D. brittonii. Stem unbranched, leaves oblong acute, densely covered white farina. Inflorescence tall, branched. Flowers pale yellow (Pl. 106).

**D. farinosa.* Rosettes in clusters. Leaves fleshy, lanceolate, white. Flowers yellow.

D. cotyledon. Similar to above but with wider leaves. Flowers whitish-yellow.

Echeveria : Rosette plants, low-growing or carried on tall stems. Leaves usually have waxy coating though some are hairy and beautifully coloured. Inflorescences from leaf axils. Bell-shaped flowers usually red or yellow. Readily propagated by leaf or stem cuttings.

**E. carnicolor.* Low clump of many rosettes. Leaves waxy, flesh-coloured. Flowers in short spikes, cinnabar, in March. Water from below as water on rosettes causes rotting.

**E. derenbergii.* Rosette almost spherical, with overlapping glaucous red-tipped leaves. Offsets freely. Short spikes of orange flowers in spring.

**E. derosa.* Hybrid between *derenbergii* and *setosa.* Very many leaves, deep blue-green. Free-flowering. Flowers red and orange.

E. gibbiflora. Tall-growing. Thick, bare stem up to 2 feet with terminal rosette of leaves 8 inches long. Leaves grey-green, flushed red. Tall inflorescence carries small, pale-red flowers in autumn. Variety *metallica* has leaves metallic bronze. Variety *carunculata* has leaves of bluish-white, pink, red, and mauve merging into each other, with large warty growths on upper surface (Pl. 107).

**E. harmsii* syn. *Oliveranthus elegans.* Much-branched shrub with hairy, lanceolate, red-tipped leaves in loose rosettes. Flowers very large, red with yellow tips in May. Good house plant.

E. hoveyi. Rosettes of long, strap-shaped leaves, pale blue-green with white and pink stripes. Flowers orange.

**E. leucotricha.* Branching sub-shrub. Lanceolate leaves covered with white hairs, brown at tip. Flowers cinnabar red.

E. runyonii. Large stemless rosette. Leaves pale blue.

107. *Echeveria gibbiflora* var. *carunculata*

108. *Echeveria runyonii*

Inflorescence 6 inches high, flowers large for genus, rose-coloured (Pl. 108).

*E. secunda. Low clump of many offsets, rosettes large. Leaves deep green with reddish margins. Flowers red.

*E. setosa. Low rosette, usually solitary. Pointed leaves covered with soft white hairs. Flowers very showy, bright red tipped yellow (Pl. 109).

109. *Echeveria setosa*

Kalanchoe: Large genus of shrubby plants, mainly from Madagascar and tropical Africa, so need higher temperatures than most succulents. Large leaves are attractively coloured. Flower spikes showy, often in winter. Flowering branches die but new shoots formed from base. Easily propagated from stem or leaf cuttings. Use a rich compost and give abundant water in summer. Full sun needed to bring out foliage colours.

K. beharensis. Large, branching shrub. Leaves very large, cordate, rust-coloured with plush-like texture. Flowers seldom formed on pot plants (Pl. 111).

*K. blossfeldiana. Small shrub with crowded growths. Leaves dark green edged red. Flowers numerous, bell-shaped, scarlet, in winter. Best raised from seed. Selected forms now available.

110. *Graptopetalum* hybrid. The genus *Graptopetalum* is close to *Sedum* and *Echeveria* and needs similar cultivation

111. *Kalanchoe beharensis*

*K. marmorata. Shrub with roundish, notched leaves, grey-green with waxy coating, irregularly blotched mahogany.

*K. pititiana. Small shrub. Leaves very fleshy, bright red in sun but greenish-brown in shade.

K. tomentosa. Small shrub. Leaves oval, thick, thickly covered with whitish hairs, tips rich brown. Called the 'Panda Plant' on account of its colouring.

Monanthes: Shrubs with low interlacing branches, ending in rosettes of small elliptical leaves, dark green or brownish in colour. Flowers, in small clusters, star-shaped, colours rather dull in summer.

*M. muralis. Leaves sooty-green. Flowers pinkish-white. Increases rapidly by leaf cuttings.

Pachyphytum: Small shrubs from Mexico. Leaves very fleshy, covering stems. Flowers bell-shaped, very showy. Propagate by leaf cuttings. Hybridizes with *Echeveria* to give many hybrids known as *Pachyverias*, with colourful foliage.

P. bracteosum. Leaves very thick, oval, whitish-grey with heavy, waxy bloom. Tall flower stem has several bright-red bells.

*P. hookeri. Leaves almost cylindrical with short point, glaucous blue. Flowers bright red with yellow tips.

112. *Pachyphytum oviferum*

P. oviferum. Branching shrub, stems ending in rosettes of fleshy obovate leaves with thick, white, waxy coating. Called 'Sugared Almonds' from resemblance to confectionery of that name. Flowers bell-shaped, bright red with prominent sea-green calyx (Pl. 112).

*P. uniflorum. Sub-shrub, height 8 inches, leaves almost cylindrical, spread somewhat distantly along stems, pale green. Flowers solitary, red (Pl. 113).

P. viride. Leaves cigar-shaped, up to 4 inches long. Bright green but turn bronze in full sun. Flowers red with large, greenish-white calyces.

Sedum: Huge genus, containing many hardy species, here omitted, for the rock garden. Mexican species are frost-tender. Variable in habit from trailing to tall shrubs. Leaves of many lovely colours. Use poor, sandy soil and grow in full sun to bring out the colours.

113. *Pachyphytum uniflorum*

S. adolfii. Low shrub with fleshy, lanceolate leaves crowded at tips into rosette, yellowish-bronze. Flowers white.

S. morganianum. Pendant shrub with stems over 1 foot long, closely covered fleshy, whitish-green leaves. These trails give rise to the name of 'Burro's Tail'. Leaves fall off easily. Flowers white, producing large quantities of nectar which drips off. Use in hanging baskets, but during flowering make sure that there are no plants underneath.

S. pachyphyllum. Erect sub-shrub with narrow cylindrical leaves, pale grey-green, rounded tips mahogany. Flowers pale yellow.

S. palmeri. Stems bare with terminal rosettes of glaucous blue leaves. Flowers deep yellow, in spring.

S. rubro-tinctum syn. *S. guatemalense*. Low-growing sub-shrub. Leaves cylindrical with round tips, coppery-red in sun and poor soil.

S. sieboldii. Long, hanging, deciduous stems. Leaves almost round, bluish, often edged red and turning copper in autumn.

114. *Sedum sieboldii variegatum*

Flowers in large heads at ends of stems, pink. There is a varie-gated form with large patch of chrome yellow in middle of leaves (Pl. 114). Hardy.

S. stahlii. Prostrate branched stems. Leaves egg-shaped, red-dish-brown, distributed along stems. Flowers golden.

Sempervivum: From European mountains and all perfectly hardy.

S. arachnoideum. Only species seen in succulent collections. Rosettes covered with fine hairs that resemble cobwebs. Flowers bright red. Soon forms large clumps by stolons (Pl. 3).

171

115. *Euphorbia caput-medusae*

Family Euphorbiaceae

This family varies from small herbs to large trees. All contain a milky latex which may be very poisonous. Whilst there are several succulent genera in the tropics, only one, Euphorbia, is normally seen in collections.

Euphorbia : Over nine hundred species known, both succulent and non-succulent. Most are leafless or bear very small leaves which soon fall. Many have powerful thorns. Could be mistaken for cacti apart from absence of areoles. Flowers small and insignificant, but may be numerous enough to form showy inflorescence. In some there are large, brightly coloured bracts, as in the Poinsettia. Propagation is from cuttings or seeds. Cuttings must be thoroughly dried before planting.

   E. alcicornis. Tall-growing, branched from base up. Lowest branches cylindrical, next triangular, and then upper ones flat. Stems green with grey edges and short dark spines.

116. *Euphorbia meloformis*

*E. caput-medusae. Low central head with radiating branches, cylindrical and serpentine, up to 30 inches long, grey-green. Flowers whitish, numerous at tips of young branches (Pl. 115).

*E. echinus. Shrub, freely branched from base. Stems six- or seven-sided, 2 inches thick, dull green with small reddish spines in pairs.

E. globosa. Low sub-shrub. Branches in globular joints at base, but young ones elongated. Inflorescences on long stems which become woody, persistent, and spiny.

E. meloformis. Globular with prominent ribs. Deep green with reddish, transverse bands. Short, much-forked inflorescences, later become spines (Pl. 116).

*E. milii syn. *E. splendens.* Thorny shrub with pale green, leathery leaves. Flowers small, with two scarlet bracts, produced

117. *Euphorbia
obesa*

almost throughout year. Known as 'Crown of Thorns'. Should
not be dried out but kept warm in winter.

E. obesa. Globular when young with eight ribs, broad and not
very prominent. Columnar with age. Pale grey-green with reddish
longitudinal stripes (Pl. 117). Male and female flowers come on
different plants. Propagated only from seed.

*E. resinifera. Freely branching from base. Stems thick, four-
angled, and spiny. Easy.

*E. submammillaris. Branching shrub. Stems with five to eight
angles covered with small teeth. Inflorescences crowded at tips of
branches, dull red.

Family Liliaceae

Besides many well-known bulbous plants the Lily Family contains numerous succulent rosette plants, mainly from South Africa.

Aloe: Very large and varied genus, from 3-inch hummocks to trees reaching up to 30 feet. They have rosettes of succulent

118. *Aloe humilis*

leaves, sometimes toothed, solitary, or suckering. Flowers in racemes of red, orange, yellow, or pink, very showy, produced from leaf axils so that leaf rosette persists. Use fairly rich compost and plenty of water in summer. If kept too dry, ends of leaves blacken. Propagate by offsets or seeds.

A. arborescens. Bush up to 6 feet. Leaves long, toothed, sword-shaped, somewhat recurved, medium green. Tubular red flowers in winter.

A. aristata. Stemless, soon forming large clumps of offsets. Leaves fleshy, grey-green, with short white spines, undersides

175

119. *Aloe mitriformis*

covered with small white tubercles. Scarlet flowers in spikes, in spring, on small plants. In winter, rosettes close up into tight balls.

*A. brevifolia. Stem short with close rosettes of glaucous leaves, 3 inches long, edged by white spines. Some spines on surface of leaves. Flowers red.

*A. ferox. Tall when adult but young plants handsome. Leaves thick, broad, covered sharp, spiny teeth on both sides and along edges. Pale red flowers in compact pyramid in April.

A. humilis. Very dwarf. Suckers freely. Leaves erect, somewhat

120. *Aloe variegata*

incurved, blue, covered with small. teeth. Flowers coral red. Very
variable species (Pl. 118).

A. mitriformis. Tall-growing. Leaves thick, green, spoon-
shaped with white thorny teeth at edges, united at bases in pairs.
Flowers scarlet (Pl. 119).

A. plicatilis. Shrub, stems repeatedly branched. Leaves rather
thin, strap-shaped, grey-green with horny edge, arranged in two
rows like leaves of book.

A. variegata. Stemless rosette of stiff, erect leaves keeled like

177

121. *Gasteria liliputana*

a boat, dark green with oval, whitish markings forming irregular transverse bands, giving rise to name, 'Partridge Breast Aloe'. Reddish flowers in spikes, spring. Good house plant (Pl. 120).

Other good species are *A. concinna*, *A. greenii*, **A. saponaria*, **A. striata*, and *A. veris*.

Gasteria : Large genus of mainly stemless plants, suckering freely. The strap-shaped leaves are usually in two rows, but may be arranged spirally. Tall flower stems carry red or pink hanging bells, inflated at base, on one side of stem. Propagation best by offsets or leaf cuttings. Seeds, unless collected in wild, usually hybridized. Few plants offered for sale are true species.

*C. colubrina. Leaves in spiral, over 1 foot high with age. Leaves wedge-shaped, dark green, with oval, coalescing white markings.

G. liliputana. Smallest of genus. Stemless. Leaves 2 inches long, somewhat spirally arranged, pointed, dark green, heavily flecked white (Pl. 121).

*G. maculata. Leaves fleshy, strap-shaped, up to 8 inches long, shining dark green, white marks coalescing to form transverse bands.

*G. verrucosa. Leaves long and narrow, tapering to a point, arranged in pairs one above the other. Heavily covered with greyish-white tubercles.

Haworthia : Large genus of over one hundred and fifty species and many varieties from South Africa. Usually form clusters of stemless rosettes, but some are columnar with closely overlapping leaves. Leaves often covered with white tubercles or may be windowed or entirely translucent. Long inflorescences carry inconspicuous white flowers which, magnified, resemble trumpet lilies. In nature they grow in the shade of bushes, so give half-shade here. Easily propagated by offsets.

*H. coarctata. Rosettes elongated into 8-inch stems. Leaves fleshy, triangular, clasping stem, dark green with small white tubercles in longitudinal rows.

*H. cymbiformis. Large clusters of stemless rosettes. Leaves extremely fleshy, thickened at ends which taper abruptly, pale green, windowed at tips.

179

122. *Haworthia margaritifera*

H. fasciata. Stemless rosettes with many offsets. Leaves triangular lanceolate, shiny dark green with white tubercles in longitudinal bands.

H. limifolia. Leaves triangular, broad at base, almost black with many raised, wavy, transverse lines. Needs care with water.

H. margaritifera. Solitary, large rosettes. Leaves erect, incurved, grey-green with large, round, pearly tubercles (Pl. 122).

H. papillosa. Large solitary rosettes, leaves incurved, pointed, grey-green, reddish in sun, with many prominent white warts (Pl. 123).

123. *Haworthia papillosa*

124. *Haworthia sessiliflora*

H. reinwardtii. Elongated rosettes up to 6 inches. Leaves triangular, incurved, grey-green with transverse rows of white tubercles on back.

H. sessiliflora. Clustering stemless rosettes; leaves thick, pointed, smooth, pale green, with longitudinal transparent lines (Pl. 124).

H. tessellata. Spreading clusters of stemless rosettes. Leaves very fleshy, triangular, somewhat recurved, almost transparent on upper surface with tessellation of dark veins (Pl. 125).

H. truncata. Leaves in two rows, erect and truncate at top, almost buried, with window to allow passage of light. *H. maughanii* is similar but with square instead of oblong leaves. Both need warmth and little water.

125. *Haworthia tessellata*

Index